Satir Step by Step

Satir
Step by Step

A Guide to Creating Change in Families

Virginia Satir
& Michele Baldwin

Science and Behavior Books, Inc.
Palo Alto, California 94306

Library of Congress Card Number 83–051128
ISBN 0–8314–0068–4

Designed and Illustrated by Bill Yenne

Edited by Rain Blockley and Susan Garratt

Indexed by Susan Garratt

Contents

Preface by Virginia Satir

My first book, *Conjoint Family Therapy,* was published in 1964. It was a response to an urgent request from the National Institute of Mental Health, which funded the last five years of the program for family therapy training I developed and taught at the Mental Research Institute in Palo Alto, California. The apparent rationale for this request was that what I was doing was important and needed to be written down.

All I was doing then was new and maybe even freakish. When *Conjoint* was published, I had been seeing families for thirteen years in private practice. The first seven years of this period were in Chicago. At the request of Dr. Kalman Gyarfas, superintendent of Chicago State Hospital, I spent three years pioneering family therapy training in the Illinois State Psychiatric Residency program. Dr. Gyarfas was dedicated to bringing in the family context to deepen the residents' appreciation of the family in relation to patients. Dr. Harold Visotsky and I teamed up to do this work.

Much has happened in the thirty-odd years since I began seeing families. Much of what I did then, which seemed so far out, is commonplace today. Other people joined the pioneering ranks, among them Nathan Ackerman, Murray Bowen, and Don Jackson.

In those early years, though, the only approach to a psychiatric patient was via the medical model. This concerned itself only with the individual patient. I did not think it worked well, and I had an intuitive sense that there were other ways. I set out to find some.

I was steeped in and understood the concepts and approaches of psychology, psychiatry, and social work, but their models were of little help in my search for clues about how people change. Since no other context or models existed for any other approach, I had only my intuition to guide me. A sense of what fit led me to experiment. It was only after the fact that I could articulate what I was doing. This continues to be true for me: my intuitive sense always precedes my rational sense.

However, my curiosity and need to make sense out of what I was doing impelled me to develop and articulate my rationale. I found help by turning to biology, linguistics, theology, physics, learning theory, drama, history, art, and play.

While I was going into unknown territory, often against the tide, many people were attracted to what I was doing and became my students. These people were of immeasurable help to me: observers often see things of which the observed one is not aware.

Michele Baldwin was one of those students. Our relationship long ago ceased to be that of a teacher and student; we are peers. I was delighted and touched when she initiated the idea that we write a book together. She hoped to make more manifest the so-called "magic" of Satir. Through her questions and her perceptions of my work, I gained tremendously. She helped me to know even more about what I do.

I owe her a great deal. She did most of the hard work. I provided only the raw material.

For me, a book is an intimate expression of its author. This book is an intimate expression of me through another's eyes. And these are the eyes of someone I respect, who has the background, the knowledge, and the academic acuity that gives this book its stature.

—Virginia M. Satir

Preface by Michele Baldwin

The idea of collaborating on a book with Virginia Satir matured slowly over the years as a result of participating in many of her workshops and working alongside her, as well as having many informal contacts. The first part of the book was relatively easy to work on. Writing Part II was quite a different story, though, and I often wondered why I indulged in such self-inflicted torture. I found that other responsibilities, priorities, and interests interrupted the flow of my creativity and my ability to organize my thoughts. It seemed I could write only if I completely submerged myself in the material and only after hours of relatively low creative yield.

Initially, I had the illusion that, with discipline and by working more hours, I would be able to continue to integrate my writing into my regular schedule. This did not work out, and I endured several months of guilt and low self-esteem. Those feelings increased my writing difficulties, and soon I did not know whether my low creativity was the cause or the result of those feelings.

Fortunately, Bob and Becky Spitzer invited me to spend a week at their home in Palo Alto, during which my only responsibility would be to write. No more excuses. The first couple of days were extremely difficult, and I accomplished little. Then a creative logjam burst, and I was able to sustain this when I went home. For two months, I said good-bye to my family and friends, spending every free minute secluded in my study. A strange thing happened: the process became joyous, ideas started flowing, my writing was unlocked. At times I felt a trancelike state, being totally engrossed in the work and experiencing great pleasure and satisfaction. I could understand how some writers have a compelling desire to create. I began liking myself again.

I learned several things. First, I could get around the inner critic and get in touch with a wellspring of creative associations of the unconscious. If I put ideas down on paper with no concern about an outcome and let them rest for a few hours or days, I could later return to do whatever necessary to improve their structure or style. I also learned that I am capable of mastering difficult tasks when I make them my most important priority. I am not very good at juggling creative activities when I have other worldly concerns. Finally, I learned that hard, lonely work can be joyous, and that when such feelings are present, I feel—for a while—in total charge of my destiny.

Writing this book was made possible through the interactions I had with many wonderful people, starting with my parents, teachers, as far back as high school, friends, and colleagues. It is impossible to acknowledge them all, but I feel grateful to live in a world where I can resonate with others.

In the last two years, I received great support and encouragement from a number of members of the Avanta Network, and I would like to thank the following Avantans for their suggestions: John Banmen, Fred and Bunny Duhl, Maria Gomori, Jane Levenberg-Gerber, Bill and Karen Kelly, Johanna Schwab, Jackie Schwartz, and Brenda Wade-Hazelwood. Ken Block, in addition to his support, agreed to make comments about the manuscript, some of which led to revisions.

I am thankful to Spencer Johnson for his early encouragement and for his ability to reframe my attitude from "I have to write" to "I get to write." To Beverly

Rowley for many practical suggestions that she may not even remember; to Grant Miller and Linda Peterson for loving me through bad weather; to Mary Clare Sweeney for her willingness to type and retype many drafts, sometimes on very short notice.

Finally, there are a few people without whom this book would never have come to life:

Bob and Becky Spitzer, who gave me guidance, opened their home to me when I was at my worst, and never doubted that I could do it;

Rain Blockley, whose editorial comments prodded me to make my thinking more precise and whose positive response and encouragement made me feel good about myself;

Bud Baldwin, who always stimulates my thoughts and my dreams, my most supportive and loving friend even when he is critical. He had to suffer through my low moments and somehow managed to keep his discouragement to himself, most of the time. I also owe a lot to him and to our daughters, Lisa and Mireille, for giving me direct experience about the complexities and rewards of family life.

Finally Virginia, my teacher, friend, colleague. Through the years, my appreciation and love for her have deepened and broadened through better and through worse. Collaborating on this book has been a rewarding experience, and we have accomplished a task together that neither of us could have accomplished alone.

—Michele Baldwin

Part I
Practice

Introduction

Any serious observer of Virginia Satir's work knows that behind her therapeutic artistry lies a solid appreciation of family processes, based on years of experience with thousands of families. *The Structure of Magic* by Richard Bandler and John Grinder contributed greatly to the demystification of her work by making explicit how her skill with language predictably helps people to change. By now, a number of her students and colleagues have integrated her approaches into their own work. In addition, Virginia has presented her ideas and concepts in several books—*Conjoint Family Therapy, Peoplemaking, Your Many Faces, Self-Esteem,* and *Helping Families to Change*—as well as anthologies and articles. As a result, many professionals and lay people are acquainted with many of her concepts.

This book intends to further the reader's understanding of the reasons behind Virginia's interventions and of what goes on in her mind while she decides a certain intervention or selects a particular phrase. Part I focuses on a step-by-step analysis of part of a therapeutic session she had with a family. Part II demonstrates how Virginia's therapeutic ideas derive from her overall view of the world. Although this book is intended to stand on its own, it touches on some of the basic concepts described in depth in *Conjoint* and *Peoplemaking.* Readers new to these concepts may find it useful to refer to these two books.

The interview transcribed in Part I Practice took place at a two-day workshop in family therapy conducted for the chaplains, psychiatrists, psychologists, and social workers of one of the branches of the U.S. armed services. A family in long-term therapy with one of the chaplains agreed to participate; the five children attended the second day of the workshop, during which the demonstration was conducted.

This family originally went into therapy because of the parents' difficulties in managing their children and the tense atmosphere of their family life. While not limited to families in the armed forces, the conflict experienced by this family often appears when a parent's career involves repeated separation from and reentry into the family.

Some concern has been expressed about exposing a family to the scrutiny of a live audience, with the possibility of exploitation, violation of privacy, possible humiliation, and exhibitionism. Virginia is extremely sensitive to such issues and does not work in front of an audience with a reluctant family. Since her main goal is to raise the self-esteem of family members, she studiously avoids responses that contribute to humiliating or lowering the self-worth of any family member. Also, she is careful not to go beyond any boundaries of privacy that family members set for themselves. In that respect, the only difference between working in front of an audience and working in a more private setting is that in the former, Virginia may make some of her interventions more explicit to the family.

She has a rare ability to universalize human experience in such a way that audience members, even if they cannot relate to the specific event, can usually relate to the feelings associated with the event and feel empathy for the concerns and pains experienced by family members. Similarly, any tendency toward exhibitionism on the part of a family member usually disappears rapidly in the face of the quality of realness that emerges from interactions with Virginia.

Although she is no longer engaged in the regular practice of family therapy, most of Virginia's approaches evolved as a result of her experiences as a practitioner. The family sessions she conducts now are usually limited in time and might lead to a false impression that she is not collecting sufficient data for an in-depth understanding of the family. But she is a firm believer in obtaining as much information as possible about the family and sometimes goes back several generations to learn about the families of origin, even for an intervention as limited as the one she conducts in this book. Also, given her vast experience in this domain, she frequently derives a great deal of information about family dynamics from relatively little data.

The beliefs underlying Virginia's approach to therapy and change, described at the start of Part II, Theory provide the conceptual framework from which her therapeutic model emanates. They help clarify her goals, described in chapter 2, and form the basis for how and where she focuses her assessment and interventions, chapter 3. These three chapters help to explain how she developed her Human Validation Process Model, which is detailed in chapter 4. Chapter 5 focuses on the family therapist as a person and a professional, making it clear that Virginia's process of therapy can be used only by those who share her basic values about people and change. The last chapter, on tools and techniques, presents some specific activities often used by Virginia and makes it clear that their effective use depends on understanding the broader context of her work.

Part II can be read first if the reader so wishes. It sets the framework for the family interview and is presented second only because we thought readers might find it easier to familiarize themselves with the session before reading about the theory.

Virginia Satir wrote the last short section entitled Conclusion as it brings together many learnings from the family interview in Part I and from the beliefs that underlie Virginia's approach to therapy and change.

For ease of reading, he and his are being used in their neutral form, referring to he and she and to his and hers.

A Family Interview

Family Members

Casey	Margie
Adult male/	Adult female/
husband/father	wife/mother
35	34

15 Susie
13 Betty
12 Coby (male)
twins { 10 Lisa
{ 10 Lucy

In this interview the following format has been used: on the left page is a verbatim transcript of the videotape of the family interview. The right page consists of observations and comments on the therapeutic process as it unfolds. The reader may find it easier to go straight through the interview the first time in order to get a better sense of the flow.

1. **VIRGINIA** (*looking at the audience*): How about Casey and Margie and Lucy and Lisa and Coby and Betty . . . I remembered! Susie . . . oh, I missed one. Come on up—any chair you like—and we can move it around. Nothing's in concrete. (*After they are seated:*) By the way, how do you sit at your table when you all sit down to eat? How is that? Who sits where?

MARGIE: He sits at one end and I sit at the other.

2. **VIRGINIA:** Daddy over here and Mommy over there. All right now, there are several kids. Who has got the place beside Daddy?

COBY: Me and my sister Betty.

VIRGINIA: All right, so you are kind of sitting like you might be at the table a little . . . and then . . .

MARGIE: One of the twins is here.

VIRGINIA: Which one?

MARGIE: Lucy or Lisa.

VIRGINIA: Wait a minute now, which one . . . ?

MARGIE: Lucy and Lisa.

VIRGINIA: Lucy and Lisa . . . one on each side of you?

MARGIE: Right, and then Susie.

1. From the very beginning, Virginia creates a climate of informal and relaxed friendliness by giving family members a sense that they are in charge of their sitting arrangements. She also indicates that once people sit, they still will be able to change their mind if they wish.

2. Virginia starts with a very human, low-key question relating to one activity of the family. She deliberately stays away from the problem that brought the family in, because her foremost concern is to develop a safe, trusting atmosphere. By observing how family members respond to the opening question, the therapist obtains information on several areas of family functioning:

   a. Communication patterns emerge: who talks first, who does not talk; how family members react to responses when they agree or disagree; how much respect they show for one another; etc. Also, communication stances become more explicit.

   b. Rules regulating communication between parents, parents and children, and children emerge.

   c. The self-worth of individual family members begins to be manifest.

   d. The family climate also becomes manifest: how safe family members feel about expressing themselves, whether children feel free to talk about their parents, what it must feel like to live in such a family, etc.

VIRGINIA: Gee, that means each of you has got somebody. You two (*looking at Susie whimsically*) and what happens to you? Where do you sit?

SUSIE: Well, I'll squeeze in somewhere.

3. **VIRGINIA:** You squeeze in someplace! But that's the trouble! (*Now looking at Lucy and Lisa:*) You know, I want to tell you something, Lucy and Lisa. I have two brothers that are eighteen months younger than myself. When I was eighteen months old, they came along. And my mother and my father often had trouble about figuring out who was who. And so I want you to help me to figure out who is who. Do you ever have that trouble? You don't have that trouble. Do you have that trouble?

CASEY: I can't tell them apart.

4. **VIRGINIA:** You can't tell them apart. So you could play funny games. My brothers used to play the funniest games. Did you ever do that?

LUCY: We did it once in kindergarten.

VIRGINIA: Once in kindergarten.

LUCY: We traded classes in kindergarten and I didn't know what she said, and so we just found out.

3. Virginia makes contact by using humor. She is also
    making a mental note of a cue that Susie, the oldest
    child, may only have a weak link to the family. The skill
    and artistry of a good therapist depends on his ability
    to register cues which will be used only if they are
    validated by further observations.

4. By using a personal example, Virginia is putting herself
    on an equal human plane with family members. She is
    also responding to the twins' uniqueness by indicating
    her awareness that sometimes the uniqueness of a twin
    could be threatened by those who cannot tell them
    apart.

5. **VIRGINIA:** All right, you did this in kindergarten. My brothers used to do that all the time, too. They even did it when they went out with girlfriends when they got older. (*Laughter.*)

It is all right, these are human problems.

CASEY: Thanks. Give them some ideas.

VIRGINIA: Well, you see, I don't think I have to.

CASEY: I don't think you do either.

6. **VIRGINIA:** But anyway, today, see, what I want to be able to do, and I'll miss sometimes, is to be able, when I'm thinking you, to be able to say you, and not look in your direction. Now, how are we going to work that out?

LISA: Just read our name tags.

VIRGINIA: I'll read your name tag. That will be helpful. All right. Is that all right with you, Lucy?

LUCY: I don't care.

VIRGINIA: OK. You see, that is what I am going to have to do, because it would be very easy to get the two of you mixed up. Do you have that trouble, Susie?

SUSIE: No.

VIRGINIA: With wondering if sometimes Lucy is Lisa and Lisa is Lucy?

5. Humor again: Humor is a way of transcending problems that have a potential for being serious. Laughter is also a strong connector between people.

6. In this statement, Virginia tells the twins that: (a) being able to tell them apart is important to her, and (b) that she needs help in order not to make mistakes. She validates the twins by asking them for their input. She is also modeling for the rest of the family (especially the father) the importance of individualizing the twins.

SUSIE: Oh no, I can tell them apart.

VIRGINIA: You're OK on that one.

SUSIE: Yeah, I'm OK on that.

VIRGINIA: OK, Dad isn't.

SUSIE: He calls them Baby.

VIRGINIA: Baby, well . . .

SUSIE: He calls them downstairs and . . .

7. **VIRGINIA:** Do you have any kind of trouble like this, Betty?

   BETTY: No, only when I get mad at them, I can't tell them apart.

8. **VIRGINIA:** When you get mad at them, you can't tell them apart. Well, I got news for you. You know that whenever we get mad it's hard to see anyhow, so, I can understand that one. And how about you, Coby?

   COBY: Well, I don't know. I know her.

   VIRGINIA: You know Lisa?

   COBY: Yeah, I know her real good.

   VIRGINIA: And so you know Lisa real good and then you think you don't know Lucy, then it is easy to tell them apart. Is that it?

7. Virginia is gathering information on the observational ability of different family members.

8. Virginia is developing a safe climate by stating that one of the consequences of being mad is that people cannot see. "Whenever we get mad" indicates that being angry is a universal feeling and that there is no negative connotation to it. At the same time, the statement that anger deprives us of the ability to see properly is of educational value for the whole family.

COBY: Well, because she smiles in a funny way and she don't.

VIRGINIA: Lisa . . .

COBY: She smiles with her mouth open and she smiles with her mouth closed.

VIRGINIA: Those are important clues. This is a clue for you, Casey.

9.   **COBY:** She crinkles her eyes and she don't.

VIRGINIA: So there are smiles and crinkles and not so much smile or a different smile. Is that it?

COBY: Uh huh.

VIRGINIA: Say, that's interesting. That's quite an observation. That's how you . . .

COBY: Yeah. Plus an accident that I did . . . a long time ago. She's got a scar on her lip and she don't.

10.   **VIRGINIA:** So, Lisa, has a scar on her lip . . . that helps you. I've got one, too. When I was seven years old, I was walking between two horses and two guys on the backs of them threw a dinner pail and caught me on the lip. The scar is very faint now. And so I had that. I don't have a twin.

COBY: I threw a roof tile.

Lisa

9. Coby is revealing acute observational skills by stating several ways of differentiating the twins. In this interaction with Coby, Virginia demonstrates the technique of having a dialogue with somebody about somebody else. In the present situation, each twin is hearing and feeling how well she is seen by other family members, without having to respond or do anything about it.

10. Virginia makes another statement about having human problems similar to those of family members.

VIRGINIA: You threw a roof tile? Was it you who did that? Was it a kind of an accident?

COBY: Kind of.

VIRGINIA: Kind of an accident.

COBY: I was mad.

11. **VIRGINIA:** You were mad. Well, those things happen sometimes. Anyway, *(looking at Susie)* I'm just curious. Coby has a way of knowing who Lisa is and who Lucy is. What about you, Susie? How do you tell the difference?

SUSIE: Their faces and their tempers.

VIRGINIA: Faces and tempers.

SUSIE: Yeah.

VIRGINIA: OK, what do you pick up on their faces?

SUSIE: Well, to me they don't look the same. Lisa's face is fuller than Lucy's.

VIRGINIA: Lisa's face is forward and Lucy's is—

SUSIE: Lisa's is fuller.

12. **VIRGINIA:** I did not hear you, honey.

SUSIE: Lisa's is fuller.

Coby

11. *Virginia:* This information is a message that has implicit information for the rest of the family. It says in effect, "All right, we can handle the angry things that happen." I have already made two interventions in the anger. The first one was when I said "When we are angry we can't see" and the second one was "Well, was this an accident?"/"Kind of"/"Well, those things happen." So this family is getting to know how I am going to view these kinds of things. The use of humor is also helping to put this into perspective.

     Comment: Coby indicates that he feels safe about discussing an incident that resulted from being angry. Virginia's matter-of-fact response contributes to the development of trust, not only with the individual concerned, but, implicitly, with the whole family.

12. Some of us were taken aback by Virginia's use of the word honey and asked her about it. Apparently, the word honey is a perfectly inoffensive, acceptable appellation in the Midwest.

VIRGINIA: Fuller, oh, fuller.

SUSIE: Lucy's is . . . hers is just right.

VIRGINIA: Well, I can see a little bit right here.

SUSIE: And Lucy is a little more chubbier than Lisa is.

VIRGINIA: Lucy is chubbier than Lisa.

SUSIE: Lisa is taller than Lucy.

VIRGINIA: Lisa is taller than Lucy, I see. Did you know all those things were going on and that people had to put their heads together to figure out who is who? Did you notice? Did you know that, Lucy?

LUCY: What?

13. **VIRGINIA:** Did you know how people were trying to figure out how you and Lisa were different? It's new information for you. (*Looking at Margie:*) How do you do it, Margie?

MARGIE: Lisa's eyes are smaller set than Lucy's. Lisa has the larger eyes plus Lisa has a mole on her right eyelid.

LISA: That's where my mom's got a mole.

Margie, Mother

13. Virginia provides more validation of Lucy and Lisa by furthering the process of individualization.

V. S.

14. **VIRGINIA:** A mole. (*Looking carefully at the mole:*) Let me see your mole. Oh there, right there. I see. That ought to give you a lot of hints, Casey.

CASEY: It doesn't work.

VIRGINIA: It doesn't work. What stops you, I'd like to know.

15. **CASEY:** I don't know. I just can't tell them apart. I never have, even when they were that big. I call them twins. Sometimes I made a lucky guess.

SUSIE: Like this morning.

CASEY: Like this morning. Usually I call them both down.

COBY: He called both of them down and they both come and get down and then he says, "Which one of you is Lucy?" Then he sends the other one up. (*Laughter.*)

VIRGINIA (*serious*): Well, sometimes you can have fun in that but sometimes there could be other consequences.

CASEY: Yep, I've whipped the wrong one before, and then they get indignant.

VIRGINIA: Well, I don't blame them, do you?

14. *Virginia:* Now, I don't know at this point whether a
     mole is a good thing or a bad thing in this family. But
     I will go under the premise that it's something that
     can be acknowledged in the context of "let me see
     this feature which is special to you" and "how
     marvelous that you are showing me what is going
     on."

     Comment: This is another way of validating the
     person by acknowledging what is present. This
     response models for the family a nonjudgmental
     attitude about things and events.

15. *Virginia:* One of the things with Casey is to help him
     start to individualize. This is also information for the
     girls. I am doing it in such a way that they don't have
     to take a negative self-worth message from this. They
     are seeing how their father generalizes and how he is
     talking about lacking the skill to differentiate. This is a
     problem he owns. Thus, the twins begin to lessen
     worries about how he might feel about each of them.

Casey, Father

CASEY: No, I don't blame them for that.

16. VIRGINIA: So maybe this is an area for whatever . . . that there are some ways . . . and maybe they might be useful to you.

Anyhow, would you come a little closer there? You are strung out on the ends. How about you, would you move your chair here?

Well, is there something you'd like to have now that you're here, Coby? Something maybe you'd like for yourself—something we would do together— some reason you'd like things changed in your house or something like that?

COBY: Well, yes, ma'am.

16.   *Virginia:* This is another example of how I
      acknowledge what is going on and also point out that
      this might not always be so good. The statement
      "There are some ways" puts it in a framework of
      hopefulness.

      Comment: So far in the interview, Virginia has begun
      to make contact with some family members,
      individualizing each one, developing a relaxed climate
      (humor), and aiming at making each family member
      feel safe and trusting. She listens carefully to each of
      them, thus contributing to the development of positive
      self-worth. She focuses on the children because, while
      she already had made some contact with the parents
      on the preceding day, she had no previous contact
      with the children.

      At this time, Virginia has obtained valuable
      information about the family. She realizes that they
      would be quite open, based on the freedom that the
      children seem to have in commenting about events, in
      their response to humor, in the quality of the listening

      and the pride that the parents seem to have in their
      children. It has also become evident that Coby is a
      very astute observer of what goes on in the family,
      and that the whole family—with the exception of
      Casey, the father—is tuned in to the uniqueness of
      other family members.
          A high level of trust has developed rapidly, which
      allows Virginia to move on to the next sequence of
      this session. The information obtained thus far gives
      Virginia a sense of how much risk she can take with
      this family and at what speed she will be able to
      proceed.
          Because Virginia feels that these family members
      share a high level of safety and trust, she is now free
      to move on and to focus on the reason for which the
      family came.

17. **VIRGINIA:** What would you say, honey?

COBY: Something that would be changed in our house.

VIRGINIA: About how you live or anything like that?

COBY: Well, you know, we fight a lot, and our family don't get along very good, but once we talk to each other in a group in our living room . . . my dad will call family discussion and everything. But then when we do something wrong, my dad, he'll start getting angry and then he'll calm down after a while and he'll yell at us and give us probably a little spanking and send us to our room or something. It don't seem right. He should stop his temper—think of what he's doing before he yells and everything.

18. **VIRGINIA:** Let me see now if I hear you. That if your father—if I'm hearing this—some way that he brings out his thoughts . . . He gets over-angry, you feel, or something like that?

COBY: Yes, ma'am.

VIRGINIA: Some way—and you're saying if he could find some way to treat that differently—is that what you hope for?

COBY: Well, yes, ma'am, but you know, he loses his temper too easy.

VIRGINIA: I see.

17. *Virginia:* It is very clear that I see Coby as the leader in the observation state. He is the one who knows the most about what goes on in this family. He is also the one that can open up things and so I use him as a lead often. And I notice this is fine with his father and fine with his mother.

   Comment: Notice the positive emphasis which Virginia uses here as in any other interview: "What would you want?" and "What are your hopes?" or "What would you like to see happen as a result of coming here?" instead of "What problem do you see?" or "What is your problem?"

18. *Virginia:* Here I was aware of the love this child had for his father. And that said to me that if a father could inspire that kind of love, there was also much gentleness underneath and that what must be coming off was his defense against feeling that he didn't count. I saw all of that in this little interchange.

   Listening to Coby, I also knew that he would not take the risk of talking the way he did so quickly if there wasn't some leeway for the rule of freedom to comment. And he also told me that his father was not always angry, and that there was a whimsical quality to his anger. This reinforced for me the feeling that the father was struggling for power and that he was often unaware of what he was doing. He wanted to be the head of the family but he wasn't and felt weak.

   Comment: Virginia's observation is based not only on words but also on the nonverbal communication between father and son.

COBY: If he can hold it back and try to talk to us instead of yelling and screaming and everything.

19. **VIRGINIA:** I see. So sometimes you think your father thinks you do something, and then you don't do it, and then you don't know how to tell him or he doesn't hear you, or something like that? Is that what you're saying?

COBY: Yes, ma'am.

20. **VIRGINIA:** OK. Tell me something, Coby. Do you know what it feels like to be angry?

COBY: I don't know.

21. **VIRGINIA:** See, I'm just wondering. You're the only boy among all these girls. You've got one, two, three, four sisters.

MARGIE: What happens when you lose your temper, Coby?

COBY: I beat on 'em.

BETTY: He beats on the twins.

19. During this interaction with Coby, Virginia gives a good example of reframing a statement that blames the father into one that makes the process acceptable. Note how the word temper has been changed to "way of bringing out his thoughts." Reframing is a technique that diffuses negative feelings. No judgment is made about the content, only about the process.

20. By asking Coby about his own anger, Virginia is beginning to inquire about how other people in the family are responding to their own anger. This cuts down on the scapegoating of the father, who so far appears to be the villain, by pointing out that Coby, too, has to deal with his feelings of anger. Virginia frequently uses the approach of checking out what other family members know about a specific feeling or problem.

21. Virginia uses a conspiratorial tone with Coby. It conveys to Coby that it would be very normal to have angry feelings at times about his unique position in the family.

22. **VIRGINIA:** OK, well, what I'm trying to get at here is that you're talking about how you think maybe your daddy could do differently with his temper, and I think we all have to struggle with that. I was wondering if you knew anything about what it feels like to get angry. I guess sometimes that happens with your sisters—is that right? Who among your sisters do you find that you really *whoosh* (*raising her fist*) once in a while?

COBY: My oldest sister.

VIRGINIA: Are you talking about Susie?

COBY: Susie and Lisa.

VIRGINIA: So sometimes they know how to get your goat? You know what that means? OK. Now, would you like to change anything about that? You'd like to somehow have your dad look at this a little differently—what about you, for yourself?

23. **COBY:** For myself—would I like to change it?

VIRGINIA: Yeah. Is there anything you'd like to change or would you like to change the fact that sometimes you beat on these characters here?

COBY: I wish that I was older.

22. Virginia is very explicit with Coby about what she is trying to accomplish, again emphasizing the universality of the feeling of anger.

23. The exploration of anger which Virginia has started in the above interactions needs to be done at some point in working with a family. It will not usually occur so early, but it is essential for the therapist to know how family members handle their frustrations and negativity towards each other. Angry feelings are common to all human beings but their expression, the ways people cope with those feelings, often make the difference between functional and dysfunctional families.

24. **VIRGINIA:** You wish you were older. Well, I can't do much about that! (*Laughing, turning to Betty:*) Betty, when you came here today, what did you think would happen?

BETTY: I don't know. I guess we were going to talk.

VIRGINIA: You going to talk? Is there something special you'd like to talk about, for you?

BETTY: Yeah. You know, when you were talking about Lucy and Lisa—how I could tell 'em apart? The only way I can tell 'em apart—Lisa yells and Lucy talks.

VIRGINIA: Lisa yells and Lucy talks. Now is there something—and I don't know this—but is there something about Lisa's yelling that you'd like to change? Is that what you're saying?

BETTY: She yells like we're 15,000 miles away from her.

25. **VIRGINIA:** I see, so Lisa could join the yelling compartment in this family. So far I've got three candidates. Now, Betty, is there anything other for you right now that you know about, that you'd like to see changed?

BETTY: Yeah.

VIRGINIA: OK, what is it?

24.   Although the interaction with Coby may appear
      unfinished at a content level, Virginia has completed
      the transaction at a process level. By now, she has
      picked up enough verbal and nonverbal cues from
      Coby to know that she can move on to another family
      member. The reason for engaging Betty is not evident,
      but the intent is to engage every family member by
      making a meaningful connection. On the videotape,
      one notes that Virginia is now completely focusing on
      Betty.

Betty   V. S.

25.   Another example of reframing: Lisa has no reason to
      feel fingered about the statement made by Betty
      regarding her yelling. The content of Virginia's
      response, as well as her nonjudgmental tone of voice,
      have transformed the blame into an observation.

BETTY: OK, like yesterday night, I had to wash my hair and yesterday afternoon I had to wash my hair. I brushed and combed all the rats out of my hair and then my sister over there grabbed a hold of my hair, because I grabbed her neck, and she pulled my hair and I had a whole bunch more rats again.

26. **VIRGINIA:** What happened that Susie got her hands on your hair? What's your idea about that?

    BETTY: She's always getting real handy, with her hands.

    SUSIE (*smiling but with an irritated tone of voice*): What do you think they're for?

    VIRGINIA: Wait a minute, now. I'm trying to get at something here. What did you think was the reason that Susie's hands went on your hair?

    BETTY: Because I accidentally bumped into her, she grabs me and yanks me clear across the hall.

27. **VIRGINIA:** I see. So you're kind of walking along and then you kind of bounce into Susie and then Susie goes *rrrp* (*Virginia raises her hands toward Betty*)— with her hands on your hair—is that it? OK, would you like that to be different?

    BETTY: Yes.

    VIRGINIA: How would you like it to be different?

26. *Virginia:* What I am trying to do is get out of the blame and get into just the observation. To grab her is the blame. To say, "Her hands went on your hair. How do you suppose that happened?" is putting it into an observation. And the more I can do that, the more I can jog what I call the observing ego in the other person, reducing the blame and increasing the trust.

Comment: The therapist's frequent use of reframing not only increases the self-worth of the person for whose benefit it was done, but also teaches all family members how to transform their ability to blame into observational skills.

27. *Virginia:* What I am doing here is to move a damning statement into an action statement which may lead to problem solving.

BETTY: If she wants to grab me or anything, then she can grab my arm, but not my hair.

VIRGINIA: Would you tell her that? Because maybe she doesn't know what part of you she can grab. Would you tell her? 'Cause this is important, you know.

BETTY (*looking at Susie*): Next time, Susie May, you grab my arm—my arm, not my hair.

SUSIE (*sounding facetious*): Your hair is easier to get a hold of.

VIRGINIA (*firmly*): Wait a minute, now. Could you buy that from Betty? That if you're going to grab her, you grab her arm rather than her hair?

SUSIE: Well, I'd rather have her grab my arm than my neck, too.

VIRGINIA: OK. Well, let's take these parts. This one. Betty now asks you if you will buy taking her arm instead of her hair. What do you say to that?

SUSIE: OK.

VIRGINIA: Now it looks like you've got a bargain you want to make with Betty.

SUSIE: OK.

VIRGINIA: Would you give her the bargain you have?

SUSIE: Uh huh.

Susie

VIRGINIA: Would you ask her?

SUSIE: I'm talking to you. Stop pulling my neck.

VIRGINIA: What would you like her to pull instead?

SUSIE (*laughing*): Nothing, really. Nothing, really.

28. **VIRGINIA:** OK, so then Susie is giving you something you can grab—her arm. That's a bargain she made. I'm already beginning to get an idea that there are short fuses in this family. You know what a short
29. fuse is? Well, (*addressing Casey*) you know more about fuses than I do, why don't you explain to Betty what a short fuse is?

CASEY: That means that it doesn't take much to set your temper off.

BETTY: Who, me? I don't lose my temper very often.
(*Family members laugh at Betty's response.*)

VIRGINIA: Well, I'm talking about the whole family. There seems to be a short fuse.
(*Family group talk.*)

VIRGINIA: Anyway, I want to find out about the bargains, 'cause we got half of it made.

BETTY: Susie, your bargain's made. You'd better not pull my hair. I won't touch you, you don't touch me.

SUSIE: That's fine, just so long as you don't touch me.

28. In this interaction Virginia is demonstrating to Betty,
     Susie, and the rest of the family how to ask for what
     one wants and how to make bargains.

29. This is a way of keeping the father involved,
     reinforcing his awareness that if he has a problem
     with anger, he certainly is not the only one in the
     family.

30. **VIRGINIA:** Now let me be sure. You have a look on your face which doesn't—I am not sure what you are feeling right now, Susie—whether you really feel this is a serious bargain?

SUSIE: No, I feel it's serious, but I don't like the way she puts it—like I'm always the guilty one and like she never does anything to deserve anything.

VIRGINIA: OK. Then it kind of feels unfair—is that what you're saying?

SUSIE: Right. You know, like I'll jump on my brother and her for beating on the twins and she'll get mad sometimes, you know, and she'll take her temper out on him. Or, you know, my brother and her'll fight and my sister can't beat up my brother, so then I've got to break in.

VIRGINIA: Now, let's see. One of the things that you're onto is you think that sometimes Betty takes advantage of Lisa and Lucy?

SUSIE: Right. Being younger than she is.

VIRGINIA: And then are you also telling me that you think that some of this has to do with Coby, because Betty can't beat up on Coby? Is that what you also were telling me, Susie?

SUSIE: Well, my brother is a lot stronger than she is and he knows a lot more about fighting. He's also a little bit meaner. So he could take care of her, but she can't take care of him.

30. Virginia responds to the expression on Susie's face to reinforce the seriousness of the interactions she and Betty just had and to teach the family the need to check on nonverbal cues in their communications.

V. S.

31. **VIRGINIA:** So, are you telling me—and you might be, and this might be a very important observation—that you think that Betty can't get things out with Coby? So she kind of takes it out on Lucy and Lisa—wait, wait (*to Betty, who is trying to break in*), I just want to understand this. Everybody's got their own picture, so we'll see.

(*Turning back to Susie:*) So that is your picture? And if Betty could get things straight between her and Coby, maybe this wouldn't happen. Is that your feeling?

SUSIE: Right. Coby does the same thing to Lucy and Lisa. Like he'll get mad at me and he'll go jump on them, 'cause there ain't nobody young enough in the family for him to jump on except for them.

VIRGINIA: I see. So I guess if you think that Coby is mistreating Lisa and Lucy—and Betty—that makes you want to go in there and do something to him?

SUSIE: Right.

VIRGINIA: I see.

32. **COBY:** Everybody else in the family, like me and Betty, have our way beating on the twins. Daddy has his way of beating on Momma and the twins, too. And Betty has—Susie has her way of beating on the twins and we can't do nothing because she could beat us up.

31. This is a good illustration of the process by which the family therapist attempts to obtain every family member's picture of how he or she perceives a given situation. Such information, in addition to being important to the therapist, also teaches family members to pay respectful attention to everyone's picture.

32. *Virginia:* Coby exposes the pecking order and the fact that father is the one with the last say because he can beat up everybody. I let that information register and make like I don't hear it, but I will get back to it later.

33. **VIRGINIA:** I see, but now that raises a question for me. Do you, Lisa, have a way of beating up when you need to beat up in this family?

BETTY: She does—she fights back.

34. **VIRGINIA** (*firmly to Betty, looking at Lisa*): Well, wait a minute. Let me find out from her. You do? Are you satisfied with the ways you have for that?

LISA: Yeah. Sometimes when he hits me I smack him right in the face real hard and I run outside (*smiling*) and he chases me and he gets me down on
35. the ground and he starts smacking me again.

VIRGINIA: I see. I see. So you can do this first smack but you might end up on the floor. Do you like that?

LISA: Yeah, but I don't like him smacking on me and beating on me all the time.

VIRGINIA: Well, what about you, Lucy?

LUCY: Well, I don't really like fighting. It's no fun at all. It's more like if you was fighting a grizzly bear.

VIRGINIA: Like you're fighting a grizzly bear, huh?

LUCY: That's me. I don't know how to fight very well. My mom and dad never taught me.

VIRGINIA: To fight?

33. Virginia continues to explore the pecking order. She
     now has the opportunity to engage the twins.

34. In family therapy, it is important to let each person
     speak for him- or herself, whenever possible.

35. *Virginia:* It began to become very clear at this point
     that these people cannot have touch contact with each
     other. When people cannot have intimacy contacts in
     a straight way, they do it in a fighting way. This helps
     me to know, too, about a limitation that the parents
     have, which is on being able to be openly intimate.

     Comment: Physical aggression is often a substitute for
     the expression of physical intimacy, which is often
     considered to be a weakness. Notice how in this
     family there is a game quality about much of the
     aggression. Parents play an important part in
     modeling for their children the open expression of
     affection in daily living.

LUCY (*looking at her father and laughing*): Well, my dad has. My dad wrestles with me every once in a while. He wrestles with us five kids.
(*Various family members laugh.*)

36. **VIRGINIA:** OK. Let me show you a picture that I see at the moment. I just want to get the picture out, and then you help me to check it and that. And I think it starts out, Coby—and this is my picture in my head from what I learned, and it may not fit at all, but it could. (*Addressing Coby:*) Would you stand up, honey? All right. Let me see. What I heard, and you can check me on it. (*Holding Coby's hand and beginning a sculpture:*) Let's put your finger out at those two characters right there (*pointing at the twins*). Swing it a little bit, just slightly. When this happens, you want to get in and do something. Now then, would you stand up, Susie? And it looks to me like what you want to do is to squelch him, is that right?

37.

36. *Virginia:* I am in the first developmental stage of this
     session, very busy trying to get the picture of what is.
     The first step for me is just to make what is going on
     manifest instead of acting on the content. I stay away
     from making all judgments by acting like a
     documentor, just stating, "Well, is this it, is that it?"
         I am also introducing little shifts in the awareness of
     family members by making connections, such as when
     I say, "There are three candidates for yelling," and
     when I talk about the fact that everybody's got their
     own picture. A transformation is already occurring in
     the process in the sense that something which family
     members put out as a negative is translated back to
     them without judgment, thus modeling for them a
     different way of hearing each other.

     Comment: It is interesting to notice on the videotape
     how mother and father are watching the interaction
     between Virginia and the children without any shame
     or disgrace. In fact, they appear tickled with the whole
     thing. This is very characteristic of Virginia's work and
     explains how she is able to work in front of large
     audiences with everybody feeling very comfortable.
     She manages to remove the negative elements of
     most situations and to transform them into a positive
     human process with which we can all identify.

37. *Virginia:* I have now acquired information about the
     pecking order and the fighting, which gives me all the
     ammunition I need for the sculpture.

     Comment: Virginia uses the words "picture" and
     "sculpture" interchangeably.

SUSIE: Yes, at times.

VIRGINIA: Well, let's do those times when it happens.
38. (*Putting Susie's hand on Coby's head:*) Would you put your hand on his head and kind of press on it, and (*urging Coby to continue to swing his finger from one twin to the other*) you keep doing like that.

(*Looking at Betty:*) Now, do you ever see anything like this? Come up here. All right now, Betty, when
39. you see this like this. (*Addressing Susie:*) Look a little mean at him. You'll have your mean look right now. (*To Betty:*) What do you want to do? What happens?

BETTY: When I get mad, I beat Coby up, but I can't touch Susie.

VIRGINIA: Let's see. You are—left-handed? All right. Make a fist. That's good. (*To Coby:*) You're now here with those two and (*to Susie*) you're trying to push him down and (*to Betty*) you're at him with a fist, but you wouldn't touch Susie. OK.

(*To Lisa:*) Now, when this is happening over here, then you get up and you put your finger out over here. Just make a picture of it—that's right. OK, keep that down. We're just going to make like we're showing pictures. OK. Lisa, where does she go (*pointing to Lucy*)?

LISA (*pointing to Lucy*): Where does she go?

VIRGINIA: I don't know.

38. Although Virginia is the artist sculpting her
     interpretation of what she heard, she is always
     checking with the participants to make sure that they
     are in tune with her. This part of the session is
     difficult to follow by relying solely on the transcript
     since much is happening at a nonverbal level.

39. Having ascertained that her initial sculpture is an
     accurate perception of what the participants feel,
     Virginia now enlists more active help from the family
     members.

Casey   Coby   V. S.

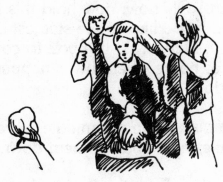

LISA: Oh, yes. I am supposed to beat on her.

VIRGINIA: So you beat on him, and you beat on her. (*To Lucy:*) When that's happening, what's happening to you, Lucy?

LUCY: I am getting beat up.

40. VIRGINIA: You are getting beat up? OK. Now, let me have you here. Let's push this chair back a little bit. Would you get down on the floor? Down, and try to bow your head, like that. All right. (*To Lisa, who has put her foot on Lucy's shoulder:*) Don't touch, I don't want you to touch. I just want you to make these motions. OK. Just hold it now, just hold like you were a statue. All right, just hold it for a minute, you're trying to stop him and you are trying to get back at him and (*to Lucy*) you're feeling all beaten up. Let's see now. (*To Margie:*) Is this any sight you've seen, Margie?

MARGIE: Very definitely. Yes.

41. VIRGINIA: Is this a sight you've seen, Casey? (*Casey nods.*) OK now, now hold this for a minute. Just hold it. Be like you're statues. Down a little bit more. Now, Margie, I'd like you to come and do what you do at home when this is happening. What do you try to do?

MARGIE: I'm in the middle. I break them up and then I take them and set them down and talk to them.

COBY (*mumbling*): Daddy does a lot more than that.

40. All the children are now in the sculpture. Although
     there is much humor for them in what is happening,
     there is also a new awareness of how they interact
     with one another. The pecking order implicitly known
     by all has now been made explicit.

41. Having ascertained that the sculpture adequately
     represents perceptions and feelings of the
     protagonists, Virginia now turns to the mother and
     asks her how she intervenes when she sees such a
     situation at home. It is interesting to note that at this
     moment there is no distinction between "the here and
     now" of the the therapeutic situation and life at home:
     the two have merged through the accuracy of feelings
     evoked by the sculpture.

VIRGINIA: OK.

MARGIE: And I tell them, you know—

BETTY: He let's the belt talk for us.

VIRGINIA: OK. I'll get to your father in a minute. You kids all take those same positions again. Would you take them back? Coby, come back and take the same position you had. Hold it just a minute. Be careful, you are trying to push him. I know there's a lot of sounds coming out of this. . . . (*To Betty:*) By the way, how do you say to somebody in this family "I don't like what you're doing?" What the "fist message"? Oh . . . (*Virginia lifts her fist*) what do you say when you do that?

BETTY: "Coby, leave me alone" or . . .

42. **VIRGINIA:** OK. "Leave me alone"—is that "don't do it"? Whatever it is . . . and you come in . . .

MARGIE: And I come in and I say, "Why don't you calm down? Let's talk this out. You lose your temper. Stop and think."

COBY: After we beat on it, you say, "I would have settled it before. I wish you'd come to me."

VIRGINIA (*to Margie*): You say, "You come and calm down" and then you try to change them. Now then, that's what happens when you're alone with the children? OK. If you sit down for a minute. . . .

42. In a subtle way, Virginia makes family members aware
     that there are choices in the way one can
     communicate "I don't like what you are doing."

(To Casey:) When you see this happen, would you come and show me what you do when this is going on?

CASEY *(grabbing Coby by the shoulder)*: I grab this one.

VIRGINIA: Yeah, you grab this one. And then what?

CASEY *(facetiously)*: He's the instigator. *(Everyone laughs.)*

COBY: He's blaming me.

VIRGINIA: I see, he's blaming you. *(To Casey:)* And you grab him . . . ?

CASEY: I take him into the bathroom and bend him over the commode and whip his butt.

43.   **VIRGINIA:** OK. Now, what if it would happen that none of this could happen without everybody's help?

CASEY: Well, I grant you that.

43. *Virginia:* What is in my mind is that Coby is getting scapegoated by his father like his father feels scapegoated in the family. I could have handled that in many different ways, but all I want to do is introduce the idea to the father that he might look at this in a broader fashion.

Comment: This interaction could not have taken place without the trust that had already been developed between Virginia and the father. He can say what he does without holding back because he knows that it will not be held against him. Since he does not need to be defensive (defensiveness contributes to deafness), he may be able to hear that everyone may have some responsibility in the situation and that he might question what he is doing to Coby.

44. **VIRGINIA:** OK, so maybe that's one of the things that could happen (*taking Coby's head between her hands and looking closely at him*) because I have the funny feeling that sometimes it's a little tough for you.

OK now, I want to find out something else. (*She motions to the children to move closer.*) Would you mind coming back? Now, when this happens and the two of you are here, Casey and Margie, I'd like to know what happens. When you're both present with the kids.

MARGIE: He takes over. If he opens up his mouth verbally first, he has it.

45. **VIRGINIA:** I see.

MARGIE: . . . And I keep my mouth shut.

VIRGINIA: OK. So how do you feel about the fact that Margie gives it over to you, Casey?

CASEY: Oh, that's the way it always goes.

44.   *Virginia:* I felt the need to be directly connected with
      Coby, and I took his face in my hands and my voice
      changed. I needed to let him know that I could feel,
      through all the laughter going on, how hard it must
      be for him at times.

      Comment: Virginia has tuned into the macho
      modeling that Casey is giving Coby. For Casey, it is
      important to give his son the message that men are
      the ones who are responsible for what happens in the
      family.

45.   Having ascertained how each parent deals with such a
      situation, Virginia is now moving into the parental
      (and marital) relationship.

46. **VIRGINIA:** OK. But how do you feel about it?

CASEY: Well, it makes me the bad guy.

VIRGINIA: Yeah, I wonder. Let's sit down for a minute, and I want to find out something else. That's what happens, but that's not what you like to happen, I gather. Now, I wonder how you feel, Margie, about Casey's . . . at least his feeling that he's the bad guy?

MARGIE: I don't think so. If he speaks up. I do discipline the children.

VIRGINIA: No, that's not what I'm asking you right now. I'm asking you how you *feel* about Casey feeling he's the bad guy.

MARGIE: Well, he does, very definitely.

47. **VIRGINIA:** And I'd like to know how you feel about his feeling that, dear.

MARGIE: I feel sad for Casey.

VIRGINIA: OK. Do you at this moment . . . (*Margie starts crying*) . . . before we go any further in learning any more, is there any way you'd like to change that? What would you like to do?

MARGIE (*sobbing*): Communicate more.

VIRGINIA: With Casey. Is this lost to you right now?

46. *Virginia:* We are now entering what I call the stage of
     chaos, where feelings are being stirred in various
     members of the family. Up to this point I was
     showing what is, making it more explicit, whereas we
     are now engaging into a process that will lead us into
     some new places. As I enter this process with the
     family, we are getting into a no-man's-land, because
     feelings are brought out which so far have been kept
     under control.

     Comment: The stage of chaos starts when the
     therapist moves into the protected areas. The
     beginning of the interview was the preparation
     necessary for building the level of comfort and trust
     that allows for touching some of the defenses.

47. Again, Virginia has to be very forceful to elicit the
     answer to her question.

MARGIE: Yes.

VIRGINIA: OK. (*Turning to Casey:*) Let me find out something. Is this something you're also aware of, Casey? That you feel—

48.   CASEY: Yes.

VIRGINIA (*to Casey and Margie*): Could you move your chairs a little closer? (*To the children, who also move closer:*) What I want is for Mommy and Daddy to be a little closer right now. It's OK.
    (*Turning to Margie:*) Could you at this moment, Margie, say to Casey something you would like, how you would like this to be different? (*She turns her head toward Casey but keeps a hand on Margie's knee.*)

MARGIE: Casey, I would like for us to have a better communication. An understanding of one another, work together.

VIRGINIA: How are you feeling as you're saying that to Casey, Margie?

MARGIE: Very soft and emotional on the inside. Deep.

49.   VIRGINIA (*turning to Casey*): I just want to find out right now for you, from you, what at this moment— never mind the past—what right at this moment would make life better for you if it could happen, living in this family?

48. *Virginia:* Now I have something real I can work with,
     because it's put into the frame of: what they want now
     is to communicate. I need to pay attention to how
     they keep going back to their rationalizations and
     their accusations. But right here both of them are
     open to the pain and the wish about having
     something more with each other. After this, there
     won't be anything more about the kids and their
     problems.

49. During this interaction, Virginia's eyes and attention
     are completely focused on Casey, but she does
     maintain contact with Margie at the same time. Casey
     has no apparent response to his wife's emotional
     outburst.

CASEY: A little more support.

VIRGINIA: Would you put some more words to what that means? I think I know, but I'd like you to put words to it.

CASEY: Sure. When I sit down and talk with Margie or the kids. . . . Last night I chewed all five kids out for lack of doing what Dad *told* them while we were out here. When we were here yesterday, they absolutely refused to do what we had told them to do, after talking with them about it. This is not something that . . . I'd like to see if they couldn't possibly sit down and be reasoned with. Reasoning with them doesn't work.

50. VIRGINIA: Let me play back, just so I know if I understand. Part of this piece of support for you would be if your children did more of what you asked them to do. Is that a piece of it?

CASEY: Yeah.

VIRGINIA: Could you tell me about any other pieces?

51. CASEY: Sure. If I'd get out of the role of the bad guy. It's gotten to the point now where, in the majority of cases, when the kids get out of line, I just go upstairs in my room and sit down and read a book. Because about the only alternative I have left is to get a belt or use my hand and start whipping kids, and I'm tired of whipping kids.

VIRGINIA: I want to share something with you.

50. The advantages of playback are numerous: it tells the
person that he was heard, gives him a sense that what
he says was important, and gives him a chance to
make a correction if he is misunderstood. It also
allows the therapist to check on his understanding of
the situation. In this situation, it is interesting to see
how Virginia feeds back the meaning very accurately
but at the same time manages to remove the blaming
element from it.

51. *Virginia:* This is a response to what I said before, that
there are some other ways. He is trying to tell me
how desperate he feels about where he is in this
family, and how he does not want to beat these kids.
The piece he has not said is that he is doing it to
please his wife, and this puts her in a power position
over him. When he says, "At this point I go off to my
room," she hears this as his not wanting to participate
and not as an act of desperation.

MARGIE (*interrupting*): How do you approach them, Casey? What is your manner? What is your tone of voice, when you talk to them?

52. **VIRGINIA:** Hold it one second, here. I have a picture I want to share with you. (*To Casey:*) I heard you say that this started out with you trying to please Margie. That is, you would come home and Margie would say do something to the kids because they haven't done well. Whatever. This is what I heard you say before. Did I hear you correctly?

    CASEY: Yes.

53. **VIRGINIA:** Now, I'm curious about something. What would you do if you stopped trying to please Margie on this and deal with your fathering of the children the way you wanted to?

    CASEY: Well, I'll tell you one thing, I've done that. I've had Coby and Betty for a couple of months by themselves, and during that two- or three-month period of time I don't think I had to whip them but once, and that was a case of necessity. We sat down and talked quite a bit more and the kids were . . . I could talk with Coby and Betty, and they would listen and they were reasonable. As a matter of fact, I learned quite a bit about Coby. I found out that he had a pretty good head on his shoulders.

54. **VIRGINIA:** It feels to me like you are giving him an admiring message.

    CASEY: Yeah! I told him then, when it happened.

52. Another example of firmness on the part of Virginia. It is unclear whether Virginia stopped Margie because she wanted to pursue her own line of thought with Casey, or if she did so because Margie had returned to a blaming mode.

53. Virginia is letting Casey know that she is not buying into the picture given by Margie as well as by himself that he is not a good father. She introduces hope by pointing out to Casey that he may not know of better ways of doing his fathering.

54. Casey seems to have a difficult time in making direct compliments. Virginia reframes his positive statement into a direct message.

MARGIE: But they don't do this anymore.

VIRGINIA: OK, now let's just check—see, you've lived with this a long time, and I need to get the pieces in order to make some maybe new connections. Were you able to observe or to know that when Coby and Betty were with Casey it was different for them and him?

MARGIE: They said it was. Like, he'd get up five or six in the morning, have them in the bed and talk to them, but he does not do this anymore. He doesn't have time for them. He's either tired—he doesn't want to take them anywhere. I know he's underneath pressure right now from school, but he doesn't stop to think about them—what they feel.

55. **VIRGINIA:** Wait a minute. Let me say what I'm making of what you're saying right now. You're looking at Casey's fathering and you're saying to yourself, "It isn't enough; it doesn't always fit."

MARGIE: That's right.

56. **VIRGINIA:** OK. Let me ask you a question. How was it for you and your father?

55. Virginia senses that Margie could go on forever
    blaming Casey about his shortcomings as a father.
    She reframes the blame by describing the process
    taking place in Margie's head when she focuses on
    Casey's fathering.

56. Our behaviors as parents are largely determined by
    the parenting we received from our parents during
    our early childhood. Unless we make an effort to
    replace those early parental messages, we are bound
    to be affected by them either because we imitate them
    or because we reject them. Women learn from their
    mothers how to behave when they become mothers,
    and from their fathers what they expect from their
    husbands in the way of fathering children.

57. **MARGIE:** Beautiful. Beautiful.

VIRGINIA: Beautiful. How was it for you and your mother?

MARGIE: Terrible. (*Laughter.*)

VIRGINIA: So you had an experience in your growing up where your father behaved differently to you than your mother did?

MARGIE: Right.

VIRGINIA: And your father behaved differently to you than how you see Casey behaving to his children?

MARGIE: Right.

58. **VIRGINIA:** OK. What are the chances now, Margie, for finding out, for you *really* finding out, how Casey would feel comfortable fathering his children? . . . and seeing how far you could let that happen?

MARGIE: I don't know how far. Children upset Casey.

VIRGINIA: We'll get into it some more, but, what I need to find out is, if you are willing to go on a search to find out how Casey really wants to do his fathering. You may not know it.

MARGIE: Most assuredly. I have been around for a while. That's why I'm hanging in there.

57. Margie's very positive response may indicate that her relationship to her father may have led her to build some very unrealistic expectations about what men should be like as husbands and fathers.

58. Virginia is attempting to have Margie focus on Casey as he is, rather than dealing with the expectations she has of him based on her experience with her own father. The blame is being reframed into searching for information.

VIRGINIA: OK, but to really find out—and even if it's different from yours, if you could hear about him.

MARGIE: I will respect him for his opinion and for his feelings.

VIRGINIA: OK, now what you told me was that you had a beautiful experience in being parented by your father, and a pretty hellish one in being parented by your mother.

MARGIE: Right.

59. **VIRGINIA:** Now, I want to tell you, Margie, what that says to me . . . and maybe we can fill in the pieces. That you did not have then a model for how a woman could mother.

MARGIE: Right.

VIRGINIA: Okay, and that would say to me something else, that there are some pieces left out in your self feeling good as a woman.

MARGIE: True, true.

VIRGINIA (*turning to Casey*): Your father, how did the fathering go for you when you were growing up?

CASEY: It was like a rock in a hard place. (*Laughter.*)

VIRGINIA: So for your experience in growing up, you didn't have much of a model in that regard?

59. Virginia makes explicit to Margie her speculations
    based on the negative comments that Margie had
    made about her relationship to her mother. Once
    more, teaching and therapy overlap. This explanation
    may help to reduce Margie's guilt about not being a
    better mother.

CASEY: Oh, yeah. I was always trying to live up to my dad's standards. But his standards were higher than most people's.

VIRGINIA: What did your father do, in your opinion, when you couldn't meet your idea of what he wanted?

CASEY: He insisted that I be responsible for my younger sister, and he insisted that I act like a man although he treated me like a child.

60. **VIRGINIA:** So that was kind of two messages. Be a man, but don't be a man.

CASEY: Yeah. What really turned him on was when I started racing motorcycles at twelve, and he thought that was machismo. He'd run around town introducing me to all his buddies, especially when I'd win a race. If I fell of or something, I was the bad guy. I had to take care of my sister.

VIRGINIA: That would be like Coby having to take care of Lisa and Lucy. That kind of thing? There were just two of you.

CASEY: Yeah.

VIRGINIA: Were you always able to take care of her?

CASEY: No.

VIRGINIA: What happened when you couldn't successfully?

60. It is interesting to note Casey's similarity to his father in this respect. He has high expectations of Coby and he's very proud of him, although he seldom expresses it directly. At the same time, he is extremely critical.

CASEY: Well, then, I got in trouble.

VIRGINIA: There must have been many times when you could have felt unfairly treated as a result.

CASEY: Oh, there were one or two times. I'm not complaining. There were one or two.

VIRGINIA: What I'm getting at here, Casey—and you sat through yesterday, so you must have begun to pick up the idea—is that we learn from whatever our experiences are.

61. **CASEY:** Hmmm. Hmmm.

VIRGINIA: OK? It is not because it is bad, it's just that we learn certain things. And right now, I'm having a feeling about you—and this dialogue may go on in your head—that often there's a fight between what you feel you ought to do and feel you can do.

CASEY: Yeah.

VIRGINIA: OK. And those could fight sometimes. How was it with your mother?

CASEY: Oh, it was OK.

VIRGINIA: So the one that came up most prominently in the way of your learning, whatever you learned, was your dad.

CASEY: Sure.

61. Virginia is picking up on Casey's reluctance to express
     too much negativity toward his father. She shifts back
     into a teaching mode, pointing out that past
     experiences are our sources of learning what we know
     and do. Virginia is trying to help Casey accept the fact
     that there were times when it must have been very
     difficult to please his father. Casey seems to be aware
     that his father may not have intended to treat him
     unfairly, and that for this reason Casey was not
     entitled to whatever feelings he may have had at the
     time.

VIRGINIA: And for you (*turning to Margie*) the one that came up most prominently in your learning was your mother.

What is there for you, at this moment, Margie, that is some vulnerability in you that you know about, that you'd like your family to honor, maybe particularly Casey?

MARGIE: A little more understanding and love and to help one another. This is what I want.

62. **VIRGINIA:** Honey? (*Turning her attention to Lisa, who has moved into a crouched position near her mother:*) Lisa . . . ?

MARGIE: What do you want to say?

LISA: Wanna say, "Don't cry any more."

63. **VIRGINIA** (*coming down to Lisa's level*): OK. I noticed that you came over here when mother was crying, and I wonder what you thought was happening when your mother was crying.

LISA: Everything was so sad and everything.

VIRGINIA: Everything was sad. Is that what you felt? (*She puts her hand on Lisa's cheek.*) Have you ever felt that before, in this family, that sometimes people were feeling sad? (*Lisa nods.*) OK.

LISA: And unwanted.

VIRGINIA: And you didn't want it?

62. Sometimes it is necessary to interrupt a meaningful interaction to pay attention to an emergent need. In most cases it will be possible to go back to the interaction and nothing will be lost. The skill and art of the family therapist is to make choices about what to focus on. In this case, Virginia sensed that it was important to pay attention to Lisa's nonverbal communication.

63. Virginia makes it a point to move down to eye level with a child when engaged in meaningful interaction.

Margie

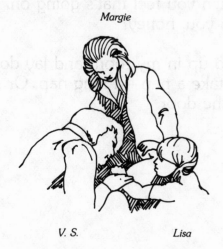

V. S.   *Lisa*

LISA: And unwanted.

64. VIRGINIA: And unwanted? Could you tell me about what the unwanted feeling is?

LISA: It's really when nobody cares for them, or anything.

VIRGINIA: Is that talking 'bout Daddy?

65. LISA: Talking 'bout everybody.

VIRGINIA: Everybody. Sometimes you can feel that there's a feeling that people feel unwanted. Is that it? (*She holds Lisa's forearm.*) That Daddy might sometimes feel that "nobody cares about me," and Mama might feel that way, and Susie and Betty and Lisa and Lucy and Coby, too?

LISA: Uh huh.

VIRGINIA: When you feel that's going on, what happens with you, honey?

LISA: I just go up in my room and lay down and sometimes I take a nap—a long nap. Or sometimes I just run out the door.

64. *Virginia:* What is happening here, when Lisa states that she feels sad and unwanted, is that she is pointing to the present but unmanifested pains between the parents. In this family, as in many others, there are rules against speaking about one's pain.

65. *Virginia:* I regard this part as a microcosm of the whole family relationship. People in this family are trying to hide their feelings of being unwanted and what they do as a result of feeling those. Casey has already made hints about his wish to be wanted in the family by his earlier statement, "I don't want to be the bad guy in the family."

Comment: Virginia, when confronted by the feeling(s) of one individual, will often check with other family members to see if they know something about this feeling. By becoming aware that they share similar feelings, family members who often keep their feeling of hurt and vulnerability from one another can begin to develop a bond leading to intimacy.

VIRGINIA: I'd like to make a suggestion to you, because maybe this could be helpful. I am going to find out if everybody in the family does know what it feels like to feel unwanted, but I wonder what would happen if you felt that way and you said, "You know, right now I'm feeling nobody loves me." What do you think would happen if you put words to that?

LISA: Then my mom would probably say to me that she does love me.

VIRGINIA: Then maybe your mother would come to you and say she does love you? Would that help some things?

66. **LISA** (*nodding*): It would just make me happy again.

VIRGINIA: It would make you happy again. OK. You're sitting down here, but I wonder if you could, just for practice, just so everybody could hear and you could hear: "Right now I am feeling nobody loves me." Would you say those words?

67. **LISA:** Right now I feel like nobody loves me.

68. **VIRGINIA:** OK. Now, I want to check out something. Since there's a . . . (*looking at Lucy and pointing at her missing name tag*). Does Lucy hear you, too? Do you sometimes feel that nobody loves you? Sometimes, in the family, you feel that?

LUCY: I don't know.

66. There is an implicit message for the whole family that
    verbalizing bad feelings may help to cope with them.
    Note that Lisa has the answer inside her and that
    Virginia is only helping to bring it out.

67. Having Lisa state "Right now I am feeling nobody
    loves me" reinforces the learning and also enables
    Lisa to rehearse a statement that she might feel
    awkward in making without some prompting. There is
    value in reinforcing a newly acquired skill by
    practicing it during the sessions.

68. Even in the middle of the most intensive interaction,
    Virginia will not hesitate to add a light touch.
    Nonverbally, she is joking with Lucy for having
    removed her name tag.

VIRGINIA: Have you ever felt that? (*After a long silence, Lucy smiles self-consciously and nods affirmatively.*) I don't know, I just wonder. You do sometimes? What about you, Coby, do you know what that feeling is, have you felt that sometimes? That "nobody loves me?" Not all the time, but just sometimes?

COBY: Yes, ma'am, I have.

VIRGINIA: Have you felt it, Betty? And have you felt it, Susie? And how about you, Casey?

CASEY: Sure.

VIRGINIA: And how about you, Margie? (*She nods. Virginia asks the family:*) What would happen if, when you were feeling it, you were to put words to it like Lisa just did? What do you suppose would happen with you, Casey, if you put words to that? "Right now I'm feeling nobody loves me."

CASEY: I have. I've put words to it before.

VIRGINIA: Those words?

CASEY: Well, nobody gives a shit about me.

69. **VIRGINIA:** Oh, that's a whole different thing. (*Getting up and pointing a finger at Casey:*) Because you know what that means—"You should give a shit about me," and that doesn't say, "I'm feeling, at this point, unloved." (*Sitting down, she still maintains eye contact with Casey.*)

I want to say something, and Coby, I especially want you to hear it (*looking down and then at Casey*) and I'm taking a big risk at this moment. (*She concentrates silently.*) I feel, and I've been feeling this for about the last ten minutes, that I want

70. to take you in my arms. Not because you're a baby, but because I think in your insides you've had all this longing to have something. (*Looking at Margie:*) And

Margie

Casey   V. S.

69. This is a good example of the difference between an "I" statement, which lets the other person know about my feelings and makes it very clear that "I own the feeling" and "I am responsible for it," and a blame statement where the responsibility for my feeling bad is left with the other person. At this point, therapy and teaching merge because it is evident that Casey is ignorant about the difference and that he genuinely believes that he is expressing a feeling when he says "Nobody gives a shit about me."

70. The nature of the risk to which Virginia is referring is two-fold. First, at a personal level she is referring to a feeling that is not grounded in adult reality and is often irrational but that activates in us those same feelings we had in early infancy when the retrieval of love was synonymous to death and when our extreme dependency on others for our survival meant that we were completely vulnerable. This feeling can emerge in even the most mature person. The mature person overcomes the feeling, however, knowing that it does not fit present reality, whereas the less mature person will be submerged by it. One of the tasks of the therapist in the stage of chaos is to help people to take those kinds of risks. Specifically, in this interaction with Casey, Virginia is making herself vulnerable by being open to the possibility of a rejection. Second, at a therapeutic level, Virginia might have overestimated the trust level that has been established. Casey may not be ready for such demonstration of feelings, and he may close off.

It is important to stress that Virginia did not venture on the lake before testing the ice. Nonetheless, the possibility remained that Casey was not yet able to receive so much warmth, especially in front of his family and an audience.

I want you on the other side. And I think for me, with you—is my reaching out into your insides for how hard you struggled, and feel that you haven't gotten what you hoped for, and I feel this strongly

71. here. (*Looking at Casey:*) How do you feel about my saying that to you, Casey?

CASEY: Makes me feel good to hear somebody say something like that.

72. **VIRGINIA** (*Addressing the whole family*): And in a funny way I have a hunch that when people don't know how to say what they want, and don't know what to do to get it, fighting is the easiest way. See, I think if we don't know how to do what we really want and we do know how to fight, that does help us a little, but the pains are great in it. (*Looking down at Lisa:*) I want to find out something from

73. you, Lisa. Is it all right with you if your mother feels sad, and she cries, will that be OK? And if you can say what you feel when that happens? Would you do that? (*Lisa nods.*) OK. I wonder if you could kind of sit over a little bit so you wouldn't be between your mother and daddy, because we have some things that need to be checked here.

71. After taking what she considers a risky step, Virginia is checking the impact of her declaration. This is an extremely important follow-up, because if she sensed any negativity it would be extremely important to deal with it right away to avoid sabotaging the trust previously established.

    Virginia again is taking the risk of a possible rejection. Only a secure and congruent therapist will knowingly allow himself to be put in a vulnerable position. Virginia is also modeling for family members the importance of checking the impact of their statements, even if it puts them in a vulnerable situation. Taking the risk of being hurt and experiencing pain is one of the conditions of real intimacy.

72. By making a general statement on the meaning of fighting for people in general, Virginia is removing the stigma and blame attached to fighting in this specific family.

73. Virginia is reconnecting with Lisa. In working with a family, Virginia attempts to have as many family members as possible connecting to the theme under focus. Lisa initiated the theme, and Virginia is now aiming at a closure with her, thus acknowledging her importance in the preceding interactions. She is also teaching the family not to get upset by feelings and to allow them to happen while also taking the freedom to comment on them.

(*Looking at Margie:*) I wonder what you felt when I said to Casey, "I want to take you in my arms."

74. MARGIE: Very warm.

VIRGINIA: And how did you feel when I said it about you?

MARGIE: Warm, and soft, and gentle.

VIRGINIA: You see, I think all these parts are here, if you all know how to use them with each other. You started to say that what you wanted from Casey was that you could communicate with him better, and what I heard him say he wanted from you was to get out of the "bad guy" seat.

MARGIE: Which he has been. I have been taking over the authority. He just sits back.

75. VIRGINIA: That's not the same, that's not the same. "Bad guy" feels like people are always pointing the finger. Let me give you my picture of what it might feel like to Casey, OK? Would you all stand up and point your fingers at your father? No. Stand up and do it. All of you stand up and point at your father. (*Everyone stands, pointing a finger at Casey.*) If he would feel that in his insides, he could feel that everybody thinks "I am a bad guy." Is that what you feel?

CASEY: Yes.

74. It was important that Virginia also check with Margie about how she felt about the intimate statement that Virginia had made to Casey. Margie might have felt that Virginia was taking sides with Casey against her. She could also have felt some jealousy at Virginia's ability to express tenderness to Casey in a way that she was no longer able to do. Again, if Virginia had sensed any negativity in Margie's answer, she would probably have dealt with it at this point.

75. In this instance, Virginia insists that they all stand up to make the blame message more powerful by changing the eye level.

76. **VIRGINIA:** Now look at these fingers for a minute. Point all those fingers at your dad. Put it a little stronger, Coby. Look at these fingers. And could you tell any one of these people how you feel about having those fingers pointed, Casey?

CASEY: Yeah, I don't like it.

77. **VIRGINIA:** That's what you don't like. Could you say what you do?

CASEY: I much prefer—I feel that it would be better if, instead of everybody aiming at me like that, it'd be better if you just came up and grabbed me and said, "OK, Pop, let's have a talk." (*To Coby:*) Like you do, sometimes.

BETTY: He don't grab you. He grabs the hair on your chest.

CASEY: Well, that's the way I feel. I think a lot of times that your temper snaps when things don't have to. All of you; me, too.

VIRGINIA: There's another piece that I felt that might be there and that's when you point your fingers—this is you, Casey—"When you point your fingers at me like in the inside I feel all kinds of bad feelings." Isn't that true?

76. *Virginia:* What I have done so far is to reshape the meaning of anger. I have diffused the scapegoating. I am beginning to add the possibilities that there can be intimacy and that anger can also have its place. When the belief in new possibilities comes into family members' awareness, they are capable of moving in areas that might have been threatening before. In this case, when all the fingers were pointed at Casey, he did not get defensive.

77. As she did earlier in the interview in the interaction with Betty and Susie (comments 27 and 28), Virginia is teaching Casey and other family members to ask for what they want.

CASEY: It makes me angry.

78. **VIRGINIA:** Are you aware that the bad feelings come, and then comes the anger?

CASEY: I've been made aware of that much. That's my defense mechanism . . .

VIRGINIA: OK.

CASEY: . . . for bad feelings, is anger.

VIRGINIA: All right. (*To Lisa, who is holding on to her mother:*) Now is it going to be OK for you to let your mother come up closer to your dad. How did you feel, by the way, Margie, when Lisa came to you when you were crying?

MARGIE: Good.

79. **VIRGINIA:** Could you tell her?

MARGIE (*looking at Lisa:*) I felt good. I felt secure.

80. **VIRGINIA:** Now, at this point you are this far away from Casey. (*Virginia spreads her hands. She is sitting between them.*) And Casey, you're this far away from Margie. What do you feel about where you're placed right now in relation to each other?

MARGIE: I don't feel good.

VIRGINIA: All right.

78. *Virginia:* Anger for me is just a response to hurt. And if people don't get to their hurt, they can't make the bonding on it. In this family all the defensiveness has been translated into anger, with the result that no one ever talks about his true feelings. In my experience, hurt always precedes anger and anger is people's most frequently used way to keep their self-esteem. It is harder to say "I am hurt" than "I am angry."

Margie

79. *Virginia:* I felt that it was important for Margie to be very explicit about how she felt, both as a way to raise Lisa's self-esteem, and also to model for family members how to talk about what they really feel. At this moment it is easier for Margie to make such a statement to her daughter than to her husband.

80. *Virginia:* See, having broken the taboo against commenting about feeling bad, I now can go to developing the intimacy. Intimacy will never be made on anger, it has to be made on a bond between people which happens by letting the hurt come out. Anger pushes away and hurt makes a bond. And everybody here is hurting terribly.

MARGIE (*pointing toward Casey, laughing*): I want to be over there.

VIRGINIA: OK. All right. Now let yourself know that, that you don't like where you are now. You would like to be in a different place. OK. If you put yourself where you would like to be, where would you put yourself?

MARGIE (*not moving*): Right beside him.

VIRGINIA: Where beside him?

MARGIE (*still not moving*): His left side.

81. VIRGINIA: You'd like to be beside him. OK. What I am learning from you is that you'd like closer contact with Casey. Is that right? (*Margie nods.*) If you were to accomplish this at least here, you could move so you could touch his knees or his hand.

MARGIE: All right.

V. S.

81. *Virginia:* I was sure that I would get a positive
     response to my statement from Margie because I was
     relying on many clues. The question for me was not
     whether she wanted to move closer to Casey but what
     was preventing her from carrying out her wish.
     Indeed, she verbalized that she wanted to be near
     Casey yet did not move. Although I thought it was
     important for her to move closer to him, I did not
     want to move too fast because then I couldn't take all
     the steps that are necessary.

82.   **VIRGINIA:** OK. Now at this moment, what stops you from carrying out your wish?

MARGIE: Stubbornness.

VIRGINIA: Whose stubbornness?

83.   **MARGIE:** Mine . . . (*pause*) and being rejected. (*Casey shakes his head, laughing self-consciously. He looks as though he may be thinking, "Here we go again."*)

82.   *Virginia:* What was important for me in the answer
      "stubbornness" was the recognition that Margie was
      blocking herself from what she wanted and that it
      wasn't all Casey's fault.

      Comment: Although Virginia is not averse to dealing
      with emergent situations when she is in the middle of
      a meaningful interaction (refer to comment 49), in this
      case she decided to stay in the mainstream and not be
      sidetracked. What was important to Virginia was not
      so much the content of the response, but the process
      by which Margie was accepting responsibility for her
      behavior.

83.   One may speculate that Margie's hesitation before
      saying "and being rejected" is an indication that after
      the smooth and idiomatic response of "stubbornness,"
      she is taking the risk of moving into a more defended
      area.

84. **VIRGINIA:** OK. Now wait a minute. (*Casey shakes his head, laughing with a disbelieving expression.*) I am going to do this, right now (*Virginia moves her chair in front of Margie, blocking Casey from Margie's view. At the same time, Virginia moves her right hand back of her in such a way that she touches Casey's knee.*) because I want us to connect. You have a wish and your wish is . . . I'm doing this on purpose, you know that (*referring whimsically to the fact that she is hiding Casey*). Uh, your wish is that you'd like to be in touching contact with him.

MARGIE: Uh huh. And I won't let myself because I'm stubborn, because I get rejected from him.

VIRGINIA (*laughing; Margie, too, is laughing*): All right. Before you give yourself so much credit, let's give credit for the right things. OK, all right. You have your wish.

MARGIE: Uh huh.

VIRGINIA: OK. And then, you stop yourself.

MARGIE: Uh huh.

VIRGINIA: OK. Then you say to yourself, I stop myself so I won't get hurt.

MARGIE: That's right.

VIRGINIA: OK. How willing are you to act on your wish right now and take the risk that one of you might get hurt?

84. *Virginia:* At this moment I want to move between them and I want her to focus on me, and not on Casey, because I am going to go into that stubbornness and that fear of rejection. In that particular couple, if I did not move myself directly in front of Casey, she would use him to activate things that would prevent her from going into a safe place inside herself, where she could begin to work at this stubbornness and this rejection. At the same time, my right hand was telling Casey that although I had my back to him, I was still here for him. It is as if my hand was saying to Casey, "I'm leaving to go to her but I'm not leaving you."

Comment: This is a very beautiful demonstration of Virginia's artistry in working with a couple. One of the difficulties for the therapist is to always insure that when focusing on one member of the couple, the other does not feel left out, or that the therapist is siding with his partner.

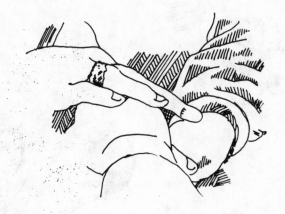

MARGIE: That's it. (*Laughing.*)

VIRGINIA: Now I want to know if you're ready to take that risk right now.

MARGIE: Yes.

85. **VIRGINIA:** Now that means that you're willing also to be told no. If that happens . . .

MARGIE: Ummm.

VIRGINIA: . . . and that you won't fall apart because somebody said no. You used to, maybe, but you don't have to any more. OK?

MARGIE: Ummm.

85.   *Virginia:* Here is a very important part. It would be
      very easy to set up the situation in which you could
      reinforce the idea that every time anybody wants
      something they get it. That is not what it is. To be
      able to say what you want and then to hear the
      answer is important. So I couldn't set her up to ask
      something from Casey under the idea that he was
      going to say yes, because that would not have fit. But
      she can make the request and then she can see what
      happens. Part of this is the risk of being told no.
      When you are little and somebody tells you no, you
      can make that synonymous with "I don't love you."
      When you are really mature, you are able to
      differentiate.
            There is an implied message here that she has
      made some changes. I try to have all my validations
      based on something that has just happened. In this
      case, Margie had just agreed that she was willing to
      take the risk of getting hurt. I know that she now
      realizes that she won't die from a "no" answer.

      Comment: The ability to view "no" as something
      other than a rejection is extremely important if one
      wishes to establish a meaningful relationship. As long
      as one equates "no" with a rejection, one tends not to
      ask things for oneself.

86. **VIRGINIA:** So, if you acted on your wish—do it and see what happens. (*Margie leans over and touches Casey's knee.*) Now what you're doing—you could make that a lot easier if you moved over here.

MARGIE: OK. Instead of reaching out. (*Margie is now sitting across from Casey, close to him, touching his knee, smiling at him.*)

VIRGINIA: Now, I noticed something. Notice what happened when you did this. What happened?

MARGIE: He kind of shifted back a little.

VIRGINIA: Is that what you saw?

MARGIE: Maybe he didn't quite know how to feel.

VIRGINIA: I saw a couple of movements and I don't know. Then you can ask Casey what he thinks he did. I saw him first move forward and then a little back. (*Looking at Casey:*) Is that what you were doing?

CASEY: Uh huh.

VIRGINIA: OK. How did you feel about Margie taking the risk of moving under her own wishes toward you?

CASEY: Strange.

VIRGINIA: OK. That's a new thing.

86.   *Virginia:* When I encouraged Margie to move, I was
      confident that she would follow my directions, not
      because she would obey me but because I was in
      touch with her inner dialogue. What I was doing was
      giving support and encouragement to the part that
      wanted to come out. I want to stress that this is not a
      technique, but a process similar to childbirth, where
      you are following the contractions and encouraging
      the mother to push. This is like the birth of new
      possibilities. When I ask people to do something, it is
      not because I am using a technique I designed for
      them but because I am in front of what is going on
      and clear on what is going on. So when I ask them to
      do something, it fits with something in them. This is
      the reason people very seldom refuse to do what I
      ask them to do.

      Comment: The point made by Virginia is extremely
      important. Because of the trust established, one might
      indeed think that Margie obeyed Virginia and that she
      might be anxious to do what Virginia wanted her to
      do. If this were the case, and if Virginia's request did
      not correspond to Margie's deep wishes, Margie
      would have been manipulated. In that process,
      she would have lost some of her self-esteem since she
      would have given the control of her actions over to
      the therapist.

CASEY: Uh huh.

87.   VIRGINIA: Now that you've gotten over the feeling of strangeness, how does it feel to have her here?

CASEY: Like it used to.

VIRGINIA: And that means . . . ?

CASEY: Well, it's nice.

VIRGINIA: I'd like you to tell her that.

CASEY: It was nice. Like a warm, fuzzy . . .

88.   VIRGINIA: How do you feel about that?

MARGIE: I disagree with him.

VIRGINIA: What do you disagree about?

MARGIE: Whenever I approach him—

89.   VIRGINIA: Wait a minute, we're right here, right now.

MARGIE: Yeah, I agree.

VIRGINIA: I want you to look at me now, and I want you to listen really carefully. There's a lot of history —I know there's a lot of history and I don't know what it is, and I have a hunch that oftentimes you don't see what's right in front of your nose, because it is all covered up with what you expect, because you almost did it right now. Are you with me?

87. *Virginia:* Although Casey responded by using the word "strange," I could tell that he was relaxed, that I did not need to focus on this response, and that I could move on.

   Comment: In the last few interactions, Virginia has carefully monitored Margie's moves toward Casey, checking every step of the way that her intuition about Margie's desire to move closer to Casey was correct. (Virginia consistently checks out her hunches and is always willing to give them up if they don't fit.) It is now equally important to check with Casey about how he feels.

88. In the last couple of interactions, Casey's voice was gentle, relaxed, loving. The expression on Margie's face as she listened to Casey was relaxed and open at first; then she lifted her eyebrows. Note how Virginia moves slowly, checking every step of the way.

89. Virginia does not tell Margie that she is back in an old movie, nor does she try to interpret the old movie. She just brings her back to what is going on in the present situation.

MARGIE: Uh huh.

90. VIRGINIA: OK, now I'd like you to look at Casey and feel his skin through your hands at this moment and tell me what you feel. (*Casey explodes into a smile*).

MARGIE: Warm.

VIRGINIA: OK. Tell it to him, because he's there. I know all this already.

MARGIE (*looking into Casey's eyes*): You're warm and you're soft. It feels good.

91. VIRGINIA: Now how do you feel, telling that to Casey? Right now.

MARGIE: Good and whole.

VIRGINIA: And how do you feel, hearing it?

CASEY: It feels pretty good.

VIRGINIA: You know, I notice something and I wonder now. . . . As Margie was talking your eyes were kind of over there. Were you aware of what distracted you?

CASEY: Yeah, I'm aware of what distracted me. I was also listening to her. My kids distracted me.

90. An important part of Virginia's educational and
    therapeutic approach is to develop in people the
    ability to use their senses. In workshops or in therapy,
    she often uses communication exercises during which
    people have an opportunity to practice their ability to
    see, hear, and touch. Most people have an educational
    deficit in that respect.

    To help Margie deal with the present, Virginia is
    suggesting that she look and feel with her hands.
    Casey's expression suggests that what is happening in
    the present situation activates happy memories.

91. First, Virginia checks into the feeling. Then she checks
    into the feeling about the feeling, which probes
    deeper. Most people are able to express the first level
    (I feel). The second level (how I feel about what I feel)
    is usually not checked into, and yet it is an essential
    part of a person's self-esteem. If my second-level
    feeling is one of acceptance, I am validating my
    experience. If it is one of rejection, I am denying the
    validity of what I experience. Virginia is asking Margie
    to go beyond the internal checking by asking her to
    share her second-level feeling with Casey.

92. **COBY** (*laughing*): That's what I was talking about. He was listening to her and looking at her (*pointing to Betty*).

(*Casey seems amused by Coby's comment. Father and son look at each other, smiling.*)

VIRGINIA: OK. All right. Now. Maybe we can take this someplace. Right now. 'Cause one of the things I'm discovering is a tremendous feeling of concern and caring from your father to all of you children and from your mother to all of you children. But I **93.** don't think that always comes through as much as it could. Now, would you be willing, Coby, Lisa and Betty and Lucy and Susie, to just let your father look at you if he needs to?

92. *Virginia:* Do you remember when Coby talked before
     about how his father would be listening to his mother
     and be turning his attention someplace else? That
     came much earlier, and at that time I didn't do much
     with it except to just kind of listen to it. Now Coby
     comes in and says to me, "See, here's an example of
     what I saw before." This is a marvelous demonstration
     of the fact that in family therapy there is nothing
     random or extraneous, it only looks that way.
     Everything is hooked together. And then when you
     find those connections, it's like the weaving is getting
     straight. And we are now moving towards integration.

93. In this family, as in many others, the caring of the
     parents is often expressed by blaming, scolding, and
     other negative messages.

BETTY: I don't care. It don't bug me.

VIRGINIA: OK. Well, it might be good, because it may be a new thing for people to feel that they don't have to be concerned with everybody. And you could have gotten the message when Casey was looking over there that he wasn't listening to you. It could have happened. (*To Casey:*) But that wasn't the way

94. it was in your insides.

CASEY: No.

VIRGINIA: Now I wonder if you could do something with those hands, to meet Margie.

CASEY (*leaning forward*): Sure.

VIRGINIA: Now when this happened, when Casey reached out to you, like this, how did it feel?

MARGIE: A tingly sensation.

VIRGINIA: Tingly. Tell it to him. "You tingle me."

MARGIE (*looking at Casey*): You tingle me. There's a tingling sensation there.

CASEY: OK.

VIRGINIA: How do you feel about that?

CASEY: Well, I'm not sure.

94. *Virginia:* I don't say to him, "You take it in a different way." I just check on his motivation. Later on I will probably be able, if I work with them long enough, to get them in touch with the different channels they use, but that's not what I do now. I have also reshaped what in the past was a cue for trouble into a comment or concern.

Comment: When people in a family favor different cueing channels, they often run into misunderstanding. In this case, Margie may rely more on visual cues and Casey more on kinesthetic cues. As a result, Margie may often feel, based on information from her visual cueing channel, that Casey is not paying attention to what she is saying just because he is not looking at her when listening.

95. **VIRGINIA:** OK. Be with it, Casey.

CASEY: It feels pretty good.

96. **VIRGINIA:** Is that a new idea? That you could be that impactful to somebody?

CASEY: Yeah.

97. **VIRGINIA:** So maybe there's a piece here for you to learn about what your impact really is. You've heard an awful lot about when you yell. You know that impact. But there's lots of other things. Here's one of them, so to know that piece, too. I'd like you, if you would, Casey, to say to Margie something you'd like from her—for her to change, some way, whatever it is.

CASEY: Stop attacking me. I mean you come on—it's an adversary relationship, babe, when you want attention, which turns me off.

98. **VIRGINIA:** I know you're talking from a whole lot of experiences. It's not very specific, but, could you be specific. In a specific way, what you would like Margie to change dealing with you.

CASEY: Sure. Like when you and the kids want to go to the park, or when you want to go to the park with the kids. Now, see, there you go, babe. That eyelid comes up, that face—the head rears back and you're on the defense. I can recognize it in you in an instant.

95. *Virginia:* That's the voice that says it's safe to go inside and look.

96. Note that Virginia uses every opportunity to raise a person's self-esteem.

97. Again, the emphasis is positive. Virginia does not ask Casey about a problem he may have with Margie, but asks him to state something or some change that he may want from her.

98. Note that Virginia stays away from abstractions by refusing to deal with Casey's global response. By asking Casey to be specific, she narrows the problem down to manageable size. This, of course, is based on the belief that if the specific problem can be dealt with and learning occurs, the learning can also be extended to other situations in which Casey feels attacked.

99. **VIRGINIA:** Let's check it out, now. You see, it might be true, but it also might not be true. You just share with Casey at this point what you were feeling when he started to talk about this specific incident just now.

100. **MARGIE:** Hurt.

VIRGINIA: Hurt. OK. All right. Now, could you say what that hurt is about?

MARGIE: The family.

VIRGINIA: No, I mean right here. This is in here.

MARGIE: I hurt. Emotionally, I hurt.

VIRGINIA: And what made you hurt?

MARGIE: Because we don't have a father.

99. Virginia does not focus on the content of Casey's
     interpretation of Margie's facial expressions. As she
     did above with Casey (comment 81), she checks with
     Margie to find out if this is what Margie felt inside
     when Casey related the specific incident above.

100. Three explanations come to mind about Margie's
     response. One is that Casey may always have
     misinterpreted this specific facial expression, so that
     each time she felt hurt he thought she was on the
     defensive. The second explanation is that Margie
     uses this facial expression to communicate a number
     of different negative feelings. Finally and most likely,
     Margie, as a result of participating in this session,
     has let her defensiveness down and is now in touch
     with the feeling of hurt which she usually hides by
     being defensive.

101. **VIRGINIA:** Now wait a minute. (*Drawing out the words:*) Wait a minute. You're back into, if you'll forgive me, into a museum for the moment. I want to come back to something else. Just now I asked Casey to ask you for something. OK? And he went into something very abstract and I asked him to be specific. Now, was it the fact that Casey found something to criticize in you that made you feel hurt?

MARGIE: Yes.

VIRGINIA: Now there's a very important point. Are you criticizable?

MARGIE: Yes, I am.

VIRGINIA: OK.

MARGIE: Yes.

CASEY: No, you're not.

101. *Virginia:* Here is a very typical point. I am trying to
       find the process that's going on, while she is dealing
       in the content, remembering some old pictures when
       Casey did not come through with something she
       wanted. Now, I could go on and talk about all that,
       but what is important is for Margie to get in touch
       with the fact that the hurt at this moment is due to
       the fact that Casey criticized her. I am expanding her
       ability to be vulnerable.

       Comment: Note the many times Virginia needs to
       bring Margie away from past problems and back into
       the present situation. Virginia's intent is to help the
       family and individual family members with their
       coping processes rather than with specific problems.
       When Virginia does focus on a specific problem, it is
       not because she believes this specific problem
       warrants solving above another one but because, as
       stated earlier, the process of coping with this
       problem can then be transferred to solving other
       problems.

       One of Margie's coping difficulties is her tendency
       to rely on what is in her memory, rather than on the
       present reality of the situation. This is especially true
       in her interactions with Casey. As long as Margie is
       unable to trust what goes on in the present situation
       above what she remembers, she will not be able to
       change her relationship to him.

102. **VIRGINIA:** Wait a minute now, you can't tell her what she isn't. You can only tell her what you think she isn't. This is important.

(To Margie:) Are you criticizable? Think about it a minute. That's not the same as blamable. Are you criticizable?

103. **MARGIE:** Like how?

VIRGINIA: Can you hear criticism from Casey? *(She nods.)* But will you now?

MARGIE: No.

VIRGINIA: What will stop you from hearing criticism from Casey? At this moment in time. At this time.

104. **MARGIE:** Communication.

VIRGINIA: No, that won't . . .

MARGIE: Trying, uh huh, I try to understand Casey, and I give way to Casey, but I don't see Casey reaching for my feelings.

VIRGINIA: Maybe you can do something with that. All I need to know right now is if you're willing to take the risk to be criticizable. That doesn't mean blamable.

MARGIE: Yes.

VIRGINIA: OK?

102. This is a very important distinction. Casey's
      statement about Margie is based on his interpretation
      of what he saw, heard, or felt. By stating his
      interpretation as if it were a fact, he is imposing his
      belief on the many possible realities Margie may be
      experiencing.

103. A criticism is a negative comment about an action
      that another person committed. It indicts only that
      action, whereas blame places the responsibility for a
      fault or an error on the other person. Criticism is an
      act of honest feedback which validates the other,
      whereas blame attacks the other.
          It must be pointed out, however, that criticism and
      blame are often confused by both sender and
      receiver. A sender may believe that he is critical
      when he is actually blaming. Often the words used
      may not be criticizing, but the nonverbal message is
      one of blame. On the other hand, an immature
      receiver may feel blamed when he hears criticism.

104. Note the insistence with which Virginia maintains
      Margie in the present.

MARGIE: Yes.

VIRGINIA: And that we can hear things and we can see where we take them.

MARGIE: OK.

VIRGINIA (*turning to Casey*): At this moment in time, do you believe Margie when she says she can at this point?

CASEY (*shaking his head emphatically*): No.

105. **VIRGINIA:** You don't believe her? And now we've got a question: how you feel about not being believed, and how you feel about not believing her? What can you do about that?

MARGIE (*after a long pause*): Talk more. And let him know that you support him, and that you believe in him.

VIRGINIA: Let me try something. (*To both:*) Your legs are crossed. Would you uncross them? And would you move together so your knees touch and take each other's hand?

106. **CASEY** (*laughing*): How's that for contact?

VIRGINIA: That's one of those funny things, isn't it?

CASEY: It sure is.

105. Rather than dealing with the content of the disbelief, Virginia deals with the process of disbelieving.

106. As they touched, Casey and Margie experienced a shock due to static electricity. The next two interactions refer to an incident that occurred the preceding day during the workshop.

VIRGINIA: Yesterday we had one of those things explode and somebody even got his fanny burned.

Well, anyway, now I just want you to be in touch here because we are raising a question of belief. I want to know now if you believe yourself when you say you're criticizable at this point. (*A long pause follows, during which Casey and Margie maintain eye contact.*)

107. **VIRGINIA:** Casey won't have the answer, you will.

MARGIE: Yes, I believe I am.

VIRGINIA: All right. Now. Will you look at Casey and will you say it to him, because this is a new step, I gather, if at this moment you feel you're criticizable.

MARGIE: I am criticizable, Casey.

VIRGINIA: Do you believe that at this point?

CASEY: Uh uh.

108. **VIRGINIA:** All right, now. What was it that you saw and heard right now that made you not believe?

CASEY: The look in her eye. The smirk on her face. Body language. It causes ambivalence on my part at that instant when she says she is criticizable, yet the message I got from her face was . . .

107.   There is an air of expectation about Margie, which
       gives Virginia a cue that Margie is attempting to
       define herself on the basis of Casey's reaction. To
       develop a good sense of her own self-worth, it is
       essential for Margie (as it would be for any other
       person) to define herself by the answers that come
       from inside her.

108.   *Virginia:* I am narrowing down Casey's answer to
       what he is seeing.

109. **VIRGINIA:** All right, will you take a risk at this point and accept that as something she means?

CASEY: Sure.

VIRGINIA: OK. Would you tell her, then, that you accept it?

CASEY: All right. I'll accept that at this point.

VIRGINIA: Now would you give her that episode, the specifics.

CASEY: OK. When you wanted me to take the kids to the beach or to the park for a family outing, the times that you chose to come up with that, invariably, were times when I had studies. Not just one book, not just two, or one subject or two, but when I had midterm exams or final exams coming, and I had to say no. Or on one occasion that you wanted to do this, and I brought this about, it was after an extremely hard week at school and I was tired. Just like I got, three days ago, after all my midterm tests and after all the studying. I slept for two days. And then I got put down for sleeping when I was tired. And it's not that I'm against going out with the family.

MARGIE (*with a hurt tone of voice*): When *do* you go?

CASEY: I don't have the time.

109.   *Virginia:* I have no way of knowing whether Casey's interpretation of Margie's body language fits Margie's internal reality. By asking Casey to take the risk of accepting Margie's statement "I am criticizable," I am helping him to go beyond his old tapes.

Comment: Rather than dealing with the content of Casey's disbelief, Virginia stays with the process. It is interesting to observe how staying with the process at times appears to lead to an extremely slow pace (e.g., interactions on which comments 86, 89, and 91 are based), whereas at other times it accelerates the pace. At this moment, Virginia is deciding that moving with the overall process is more important than sorting out the reasons for Casey's disbelief.

110. **VIRGINIA:** I want to guide this a little bit. What did you hear Casey say?

MARGIE: That he's depressed. He's fatigued. He's worn out. He's exhausted. You name it, and that's what Casey is.

VIRGINIA: All right. (*To Casey:*) Now I want to find out if that's what you thought you were saying to Margie.

CASEY: No. The times she picked were the wrong times. There were other times when this could transpire. Three weeks ago I had a whole weekend off, but we didn't go anywhere.

VIRGINIA: All right. (*To Margie:*) Would you tell Casey what you heard him say now.

MARGIE: That whenever he was off we didn't go anywhere this weekend.

111. **VIRGINIA:** OK. Now I wonder what you're feeling as you're hearing this. Right now.

MARGIE: Umm, hurt. Hurt, for me and the kids. Because they don't have a father.

CASEY: There we go, see.

MARGIE: He's here in presence, but he's . . .

110. *Virginia:* I realized how easy it would be for them to activate the old blaming tapes and go back into the museum. I wanted to avoid this, because I wanted them to be able to experience that they can do something different when they focus on seeing and hearing what is going on right at the moment. This is the reason I stated that I wanted to guide the interaction.

Comment: Virginia is avoiding the temptation of making a statement such as "See, you are playing the old tape," to which the response would be "I am sorry I am doing that bad thing again." Rather than seeing them fall into the rut once more, Virginia guides them around it.

111. This interchange offers a good opportunity to observe how Virginia checks on the message sent and received by two persons engaged in a verbal exchange: first, checking with Casey that he was correctly heard; second, asking Margie to repeat what she heard; and finally, checking on the feeling elicited in Margie about what she heard.

VIRGINIA: Wait a minute. You see, this is the kind of stuff that gets you into all kinds of stuff. I heard you say that you wanted to do something about changing communication, right?

MARGIE: Right.

112. **VIRGINIA:** And I know how tempting it is to go back into the museum. And both of you have a highly developed skill to do abstractions. Yesterday when you were playing the games you were very good— "you never do" and "you always do," do you remember that? By the way, when we were playing **113.** them yesterday, what was the one you know lots about? Blaming, placating, being super-reasonable, irrelevant? Which of those are you friendly with?

MARGIE: . . . down on the floor [as the placator].

VIRGINIA: Down on the floor?

MARGIE: Yeah.

VIRGINIA (*to Casey*): Which one did you find out?

CASEY: I told my family yesterday that the one I was comfortable in and felt the best in was the super-reasonable.

112. *Virginia:* We were at an impasse here, because it was
     clear that Margie had great difficulty staying in the
     present. This made me decide to change my
     approach, because Margie could change her way
     only if she was aware of what she was doing.
     Casey's awareness ("There we go, see") and mine
     would not help her.

113. As mentioned in the introduction, this family session
     occurred on the second day of a workshop. During
     the first day, the participants were involved in
     communication exercises that enabled them to
     become aware of some of the communication
     patterns they use most.

114. **VIRGINIA:** Those are two you know about. All right. Let's get up. (*To Casey:*) Will you please come up here and take the super-reasonable position? Very tight. Very tight.

MARGIE (*joking*): He's comfortable there.

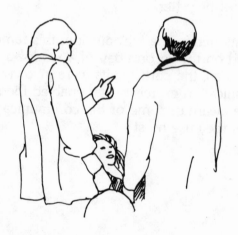

114.   *Virginia:* I am dealing with Margie's and Casey's
        inner reactions rather than what may be the "best" fit
        for them. I can only work on the basis of what is
        inside them. If Casey disagreed with the picture that
        Margie had of herself as a placator and saw her as a
        blamer, I would first deal with Margie's picture of
        herself and then ask her if she would be willing to be
        Casey's "blaming" picture of her. Once in that
        position, I would ask her if that felt in any way
        familiar. This approach diffuses the possibility of
        arguing about what is right, since by agreeing to
        participate in Casey's picture, Margie is not
        abdicating her own experience.

        The positions of placator, blamer,
        super-reasonable, and irrelevant are actually not
        fixed. Changes occur with a different context or
        when different people are involved in the interaction.
        It is also important to realize that people are often
        not aware of how they come across, because they
        are mostly aware of their inner experience. And the
        inner experience of the blamer and the placator are
        not that different. In both cases, they are
        experiencing a low sense of self-worth and a need to
        defend themselves against the perceived danger.
        How this gets translated into behavior (blaming or
        placating) can change.

115. **VIRGINIA** (*touching Margie's cheek in a supportive manner. She is joking, but the message is serious*): Now, you stop talking about what he is. I want you to be where you are. All right. Down, dear. . . . We'll do this. . . . Now, we've gotta get this really right. Oh, here, no here. . . . Yeah, but your feet aren't

116. right yet. (*Virginia is down on the floor helping Margie into the correct placating position.*) You're too solid, down there. All right, here and here and here, and the heart (*indicating that Margie's left hand should be on her heart*). OK. But, now, you see, it's not like that (*correcting the position further*), it's like that, looking up. Now, he can't see you, of course, because he's looking over there. (*Casey is standing up very straight in a super-reasonable position.*) And you've been trying to pinch him around to get him

117. to notice you, eh?

115. Virginia's comment to Margie is a reminder to all of us of how much more comfortable it is to focus on the behavior of those around us rather than on our own feelings and behaviors.

116. Virginia often models for family members what she would like them to do. Because of her spontaneity and lack of concern about how she might be coming across and what her "image" might be like, she obtains excellent cooperation. In all the years I have watched her work, I have not seen anyone refuse to do what she asked them to do.

117. This part of the session comes to life in the videotape (refer also to comment 120). By positioning Margie in a placating position and Casey in a super-reasonable one, Virginia is exaggerating a situation with which they have had experience at times. The value of the sculpture is that it allows Virginia to elicit the feelings with which both Casey and Margie have experience: Casey as the super-reasonable one so involved in his principles and his rational vision of the world that he loses touch with people and remains unaware of their feelings as well as his own feelings; and Margie as the placating one who, in her fear of asserting her needs and wants, tries to attract attention in an oblique, covert manner.

MARGIE (*laughing*): Right.

118. **VIRGINIA:** OK. That's one string you got to the bow.
(*To Casey:*) You can't see her down there, can
you? You don't know what she's doing.

CASEY: Just barely.

VIRGINIA: Now, you see what you could do is step
forward a little bit (*taking Casey's hand and putting
it on Margie's head*) . . . pat, pat, pat.
(*To Margie, who is laughing:*) Do you ever get
119. that? Feel that? Now that's right, you see. OK. That's
one line. But you do something else then (*helping
Margie to get up and to point a blaming finger at
Casey*) 'cause you do this. Follow the finger.
(*Laughter.*)
(*To Casey:*) Now, when that finger comes out, I
think your finger goes out, too.
(*Laughter.*)
Now then, this gets broken up. You know how you
break this up?

MARGIE: No, how?

VIRGINIA: How does this change for you, how do
you get from this spot to another spot?

118. This whole therapeutic/learning experience is put in
     a humorous context which enables both Casey and
     Margie to be aware of their behavior without
     needing to be defensive about it. In many situations,
     humor can give a moment of spontaneous insight
     manifested by laughter, which anchors the experience
     in our memory in such a way that similar
     experiences in the future may be put in a humorous
     rather than a blaming context.

119. Virginia in this sequence is the stage director in
     charge of structuring the situation. She bases her
     intervention on the process which she believes is
     taking place at stressful times between Casey and
     Margie. Having allowed Margie to develop her
     picture of herself as a placator, she now leads her
     into the blaming position, which Virginia knows to
     be present on the basis of previous interactions.

MARGIE: Walk away.

VIRGINIA: Well, that's what I thought you did. So the one way you can break this out is to turn your back, and when you turn your back . . .

(*Addressing Casey:*) I'll tell you my fantasy of what happens: You go down on the floor (*she gently guides Casey down into a placating position*), only you turn down on the floor, practically with your nose on the floor [and you think] "She doesn't care about me."

(*To Margie:*) And you don't know that. I mean, that's a whole new idea to you. The kids know it, because they can see it. All right. Now you get lonely over here, don't you? (*At this moment, Margie is standing with her back to Casey, who is still down in a placating position.*)

MARGIE: Uh huh.

VIRGINIA: So, now, if you don't mind, we'll exaggerate it a little bit, as you get down here (*Margie is now down on the floor; Virginia turns to Casey*) and you think about being lonely. You get down, turn around, crawling on all fours. And the minute you see her coming, stand up and be super-reasonable. (*Casey is now back in his original*
120. *standing position.*) Now you stand there for a while, and then we repeat the whole thing.

(*To Margie:*) You get up, you start to get mad (*Margie points a blaming finger, laughing*), and think of all the things that have happened. That's right. So

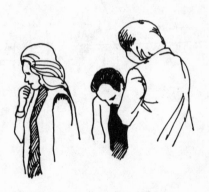

120. In the absence of videotape, this ballet sequence is
     very difficult to follow. The brief summary of what is
     described here may help the reader. The sequence of
     the ballet (sculpture in motion) is as follows:
       1. Margie in a placating position on the floor in
           front of a super-reasonable Casey.
       2. Virginia comments to Margie on the fact that
           while she is in this position, she may

then he says, "You're not gonna do me that way, baby doll (*Casey points a blaming finger*) . . . and down with that." (*Margie now turns her back.*) That's right, how can you treat me like that?"

sometimes try to attract Casey's attention. Virginia makes Casey aware of his inability to see Margie when he is in this position.

3. Then, Virginia gives Casey a process picture that formed in her head: a paternalistic, out-of-touch pat on the head from a super-reasonable person who knows that sometimes it is important for people to make a contact.

4. Virginia puts Margie in a blaming position and suggests to Casey that when this happens, he blames, too.

5. Virginia checks with Margie on what her reaction is when Casey blames back.

6. Margie states that when this happens, she walks away. Then Virginia suggests to Casey that he gets into a placating position when this happens.

7. Virginia then makes Margie aware of the fact that since her back is turned she does not know of Casey's dejected feeling of "She [Margie] does not care about me."

8. Then, tuning into Margie's feeling of loneliness and her wish to connect, Virginia completes the first movement of the ballet by having Margie approach Casey on a placating level. This immediately reminds Casey that men are not supposed to show weakness and sends him back up in a super-reasonable position.

9. The second movement of the ballet is a repetition of the first movement.

(*To Margie:*) And you go out and feel guilty and want something. (*Casey again goes down in a placating position.*)

121.

(*To Casey:*) Crawl in . . . and you can't stand that, get up.

CASEY (*laughing*): It wears you out.

VIRGINIA (*laughing*): It sure does. (*To Margie:*) OK. All right. Are you with me?

MARGIE: Uh huh.

VIRGINIA: All right. Now, you noticed there's no way in the world down there that you can meet him. But let me show you—go down again and let me show you a little tactic. (*Margie gets down in a placating position.*) Move over close, you see. A little closer. Now, if you move closer, you can put one toe on his toe. You can make trouble for him that way.

MARGIE: Oh, yes.

VIRGINIA: And then you can fall all over him like that, you see. You can fall over on him. That's right. You can do that.

MARGIE (*laughing*): Can I knock him off balance that way?

VIRGINIA (*serious*): You could, because if he's retained that position, then one of the things he'll do, he's not going to be knocked off balance,

121. A ballet is better than a thousand words. If this ballet
      had been replaced by words the inaccuracy of the
      spoken language might have led to many possible
      misinterpretations between Margie's and Casey's
      meanings, and time would have had to be spent to
      check on the correct understanding of the meanings.
      The ballet allows for an organic knowledge which
      gives instant feedback to the person about the
      accuracy of a feeling or of a behavior.

because if you start knocking him off balance, see what you do. (*Casey moves away.*)

(*Laughter.*)

That's right. You see. All right, now you're where you're into a fun piece with this.

MARGIE: Yeah.

VIRGINIA: There's also a piece that fits here. How do you balance off each other? OK. What do you think? (*Virginia has Casey and Margie standing, pointing*
122. *blaming fingers at each other.*) This is the one where the tears come, inside. But the words are terrible on the outside.

MARGIE: Yes.

VIRGINIA: OK?

MARGIE: Uh huh.

VIRGINIA: All right. OK.

MARGIE: True.

VIRGINIA: Let's come back now and let's see what more we can find out. (*Casey, Margie, and Virginia sit down. Virginia addresses Margie.*) See, from down there you can't see where he is. From up there, he
123. can't see where you are, and when you're like this (*pointing*), you can't see, either. So, when I ask you if you're criticizable, all I mean is, are you teachable?

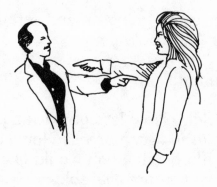

122. *Virginia:* What I am trying to do here is first of all
bring out their interactions in this. I am showing
them that they are not helpless and that they have
choices. I am also reinforcing my former statement
that when people do not know how to get close,
they fight. I am also pointing out that the price is
heavy and that the terrible words on the outside do
not prevent the hurt and tears on the inside. This is
an important connection that people need to make
in families: namely, that there is often a difference
between the outside message and the inside feeling.

123. The ballet has made very clear the impossibility for
anyone to communicate effectively when using an
incongruent communication stance.

124.   Can you hear what's going on and can you listen?
(*To Casey:*) And could you?

CASEY: Uh huh.

VIRGINIA: All right. Now let's go back again. (*Margie
and Casey sit facing each other.*) Now I'd like to
have you tell Margie that you would like to be able
to tell her when you are available.

CASEY: I'd like to be able to tell you when I have the
time and I'm available for the family to go out on a
family outing.

MARGIE: I'll accept that.

VIRGINIA: OK. Now, you've just made an agreement
about something. Casey will tell you when he's
available, and you've agreed to accept that. That's
one piece. All right. Would you be willing to ask
Casey if he would listen to you when you would like
him to be available?

125.   **MARGIE:** Casey, would you listen whenever I try to
tell you that we're available to go out?

CASEY: Yeah.

VIRGINIA (*to Margie*): Now you've made two
agreements that can make a great difference in your
life if you do it, because Casey says he'll tell you
when he's available. That doesn't always mean you
would be available, but he'll tell you when. That's a
beginning start. You've told him you will tell him

124. *Virginia:* At this point, I have retrenched from blamable, to criticizable, to teachable.

   Comment: After a long detour, Virginia returns to the point she was trying to make earlier. She maintains the focus even when it might appear that she has taken off in another direction.

125. Virginia directs this interaction between Casey and Margie with precision. The content of this interaction is not important; what is significant is that Casey and Margie learn how to become more effective in their communication with each other. This is again a time when therapy and teaching merge, since good will alone would not permit good communication if the skills were lacking.

126. when you're available, and you say you'll listen. That doesn't mean that's going to end in availability. It only means you're telling each other where you are to begin something. Do you follow what I'm saying?

MARGIE: Uh huh.

VIRGINIA: It's very important that each of you can let the other know. But that doesn't mean that the other one has an obligation. It only means you have a place to start.

126. Again the emphasis is on the use of the words yes
      and no. Only when those two words are used in
      contexts such as the present interaction, instead of
      being linked to pleasing and loving or displeasing
      and rejecting, can real communication occur within a
      relationship.

Conclusion

My purpose in seeing this family had two parts. The first was to demonstrate to a professional audience how an interview conducted by me looks, sounds, and feels. My intent was to deepen their appreciation of family process and of how I make interventions. The second purpose was to offer this family an experience by which it could increase its repertoire of coping abilities.

I proceed from the theory that my therapeutic job is to expand, redirect, and reshape individuals' ways of coping with each other and themselves so they can solve their own problems in more healthy and relevant ways. Problems are not the problem; coping is the problem. Coping is the outcome of self-worth, rules of the family systems, and links to the outside world.

Unsatisfactory coping is the outcome of low self-esteem, manifest in erosive defenses, incongruent communication, and rigid, inflexible rules based largely on deprivation and limitation. Combined, these create a disharmony that reflects itself in physical illness, emotional turmoil, intellectual sterility, and relationship tragedies.

My aim is to start the process of satisfactory coping. I engage in interventions that raise self-esteem, develop congruent communications, and provide useful guides based on abundance and infinity, our birthright as human beings.

The people in this family no longer see each other or themselves as they did before. Their work is not complete, though, and my hope is that they are closer to meeting new challenges in more healthy ways.

—Virginia M. Satir

Part II
Theory

Chapter 1
Beliefs
Underlying the
Satir Approach
to Therapy
and Change

To understand how Virginia Satir has developed her approach to family therapy, it is important to understand her underlying beliefs and assumptions about the world and the people in it. This chapter establishes a conceptual framework for what Virginia emphasizes and utilizes in therapy, and it is the logical starting point for most readers. Some may feel more comfortable reading it last, however.

Three areas will be explored as part of this conceptual framework. First is her philosophical view of man's place the world, with special emphasis on comparing the "Seed Model," an organic construct of the world, to the "Threat and Reward Model," on which most of Western civilization has been built. Second are Virginia's beliefs about the way individuals grow and develop as well as about the influences that affect them. Third are her theories about learning and change.

The Individual's Place in the World

To Virginia, the world is a place of infinite splendor, evolution, and transformation. Since they are of this world, human beings partake in those qualities. They are creatures of wonder in their physical aspects: lung tissues which, if spread out, would cover an area of more than an acre; 16.3 square feet of skin with millions of pores for breathing; there are resources for garbage and sewage disposal; and factories manufacturing all kinds of hormones and compounds, to name just a few of the many complex components that make up the body. Then, of course, people have minds and souls. For years, the "science" of psychotherapy disregarded the soul, which it considered to be the realm of organized religion. This ignored the fact that when people forget their spiritual dimensions, they feel lost because they have no connection with the life force or universal mind. To quote Virginia:

"As I have been evolving, I have had experiences which tell me that there exists something which could be called the life force or universal mind. I know that there are many dimensions in this force that are powerful shapers in human behavior. It seems a little to me like the presence of electricity. It was always there, yet it waited for someone to identify it, then learn ways to use it for beneficial purposes."

Individuals are not always in touch with their life force. Many people do not pay attention to the treasure that they are, and need help finding it. The unique beauty of a person is sometimes buried deep; much digging may be required to find it, but it is always there. This strong belief in the uniqueness and beauty of every human being changes the character of the psycho-therapeutic relationship: an "I (expert)–You (a person with a problem who needs my help)" hierarchy between the therapist and the client becomes an "I–Thou" relationship. This human connection will help the client get in touch with his life force.

A word of caution. Virginia is a very realistic woman who does not hold a pollyannish view of the world. She is aware that human treasures are sometimes deeply buried and hardly accessible. She also knows that although growth and change are characteristics of life, they do not always manifest themselves in a positive direction. Just as a cancer can grow, people's personalities can develop in ways that are harmful to themselves and to others.

What is important is to determine under what conditions growth occurs in a positive direction, and to provide those conditions for all that live. Answers are complex and often contradictory; what appear to some people to be good conditions for growth are not so for others.

In her workshops and other presentations, Virginia brings to life two opposite views of the world: the "Threat and Reward" model and the "Seed" model. These two models contrast sharply in four areas: the definition of a relationship, the definition of a person, the explanation of events, and people's attitudes toward change. Virginia states that by knowing how people manage those four areas, she can get a basic understanding of how people live their lives.

Relationships in the Threat and Reward model presuppose a hierarchy in which some people define the rules of good conduct and others need to follow those rules. This hierarchy is based on the roles which the individual holds in life as well as rigid expectations of conformity to those roles, thus narrowing the range of possibilities given to the individual. In other words, those on top—parents, teachers, doctors, bosses, religious and secular leaders—know what is best for those on the bottom—children, students, employees, religious followers, patients. Those on top are not necessarily malevolent; their behavior is based on the belief that they are acting for the good of those below. When they reprimand and blame, they believe that they are helping others to learn the right way. Besides, they also show their love by rewarding and praising those below for their good actions. The consequences of this top–down hierarchical model include political revolutions, religious wars, and rebellions. Perhaps worst of all, it creates individuals who do not know how to feel good about themselves. They experience loneliness and isolation at the top, weakness and worthlessness at the bottom.

The definition of a person in this Threat and Reward model is based on set norms of behavior. Those above establish standards that require everyone to do things in the same way. A little boy must not cry when he is hurt. A little girl must play with dolls even if she hates them. The student must follow directions and look at his teacher to prove that he is paying attention, regardless of whether he actually concentrates better by attending in a different way. The patient is supposed to comply with the doctor's instructions despite any misgivings. Differentness in all its forms is to be wiped out because it could sabotage the existing order. As a result, the individual feels compelled to act in certain ways. The cost for not conforming is guilt, fear, or rejection. Resentment and hostility are natural consequences when people behave only to satisfy others' expectations rather than their own. For some individuals, unbearable hopelessness may ensue as well.

In the Seed model, by way of contrast, personhood determines identity. Every human being is born with a potential that may be fulfilled during that person's existence on this planet. This potential varies from human being to human being, but the fact that one individual has more ability than another does not put him in a superior position. Roles and status are words that help define relationships only within specific contexts. Thus, Mary considers herself a parent only when she is involved in her parental role; her personhood is much broader, encompassing many other dimensions. Fred is a physician when he is engaged in thoughts, activities, and concerns that relate to his medical expertise; at other times, he is a husband, father, citizen, chess player, etc. This does not mean that praise and criticism do not have their place in the Seed model, but rather that the context in which they are given is not based on any permanent status or role of the giver and the receiver. Relationships based on this model can be truly loving and nonmanipulative.

In this model, every person is unique. Each is a fountain whose water is similar to other water in its essence, yet different because it contains special and unique ingredients and minerals. In addition to people's similarities (we all have belly buttons, pay taxes, and die), our differences make us unique and give us something of which we can be proud. Furthermore, using our differences constructively enriches the world. An individual's wholeness is based on an acceptance of the special way in which he differs from the rest of us.

The Threat and Reward model explains events in a linear and simplistic fashion that does not take into account the numerous variables that usually account for reality. We find good examples of this simplistic view in much of the vulgarization of research so popular in our media: "Don't eat butter, it causes cancer; eat margarine instead" (until, of course, the reverse becomes true). Such thinking leads to a model of the world in which everything can be seen in terms of black and white choices or dictates. In the field of mental health, this linear way of thinking has resulted in simplistic explanations regarding the causation of behavior and the etiology of disease.

In the Seed model, a multiplicity of variables is taken into consideration in explaining any event. Explaining events is further complicated by the fact that these variables often interact with one another. Such an approach engenders humility on the part of anyone attempting to explain an outcome, and there is an awareness that the truth may change as more variables are discovered.

People's attitudes and approaches toward changes also differ greatly in each model. In the Threat and Reward model, the fear of change keeps people preoccupied with maintaining things as they are, thus blocking the natural flow of life and creating many problems. Force and compulsion are necessary to dam the river of change, and the maintenance of the status quo becomes essential regardless of its cost.

In the Seed model, change is viewed as an ongoing life process occurring at a cellular as well as a cosmic level. Change can also be welcomed as an opportunity to move into new areas. People are aware that change offers them new options and choices that would not be available to them if they hung on to the status quo. This is scary, of course, because new areas are unknown territory that may expose us to new risks.

Essentially, these two models hold different views about human beings. In the Seed model, human beings are considered to be potentially good. This is not saying that people are born innocent or good, but that there is a wisdom to the body and that, given the proper conditions of nurture, children, like seedlings, are likely to develop into healthy adults. In the Threat and Reward model, human beings are inherently bad: "fallen angels" with dangerous emotions, they will stay on the straight and narrow path of respectable behavior only if they are given the proper constraints and threats from the outside. In other words, man is born evil and needs to be controlled from birth in order to develop as a productive and responsible human being.

Most, if not all, civilizations and many religions are based on this Threat and Reward model. Furthermore, adherents believe that following its principles leads to an "appropriate" lifestyle and promotes good mental health. One may wonder, though, about the sanity of its mental health model when one reads the following character description of a person who seems to fit that model:

"One of the most disturbing facts that came out in the Eichmann trial was that a psychiatrist examined him and pronounced him *perfectly sane.* I do not doubt it at all, and that is precisely why I find it disturbing. If all the Nazis had been psychotics, as some of their leaders probably were, their appalling cruelty would have been in some sense easier to understand. It is much worse to consider this calm, 'well-balanced,' unperturbed official conscientiously going about his work, his administrative job, which happened to be the supervision of mass murder. He was thoughtful, orderly, unimaginative. He had a profound respect for system, law, and order. He was obedient, loyal, a faithful officer of a great state. He served his government very well.

He was not bothered much by guilt. I have not heard that he developed any psychosomatic illnesses. Apparently, he slept well. He had a good appetite, or so it seems.

I am beginning to realize that 'sanity' is no longer a value or an end in itself. The 'sanity' of modern man is about as useful to him as the huge bulk and muscles of the dinosaur. If he were a little less sane, a little more doubtful, a little more aware of his absurdities and contradictions, perhaps there might be a possibility of his survival. But if he is sane, too sane . . . perhaps we must say that in a society like ours the worst insanity is totally without anxiety, totally 'sane.' ''*

The Threat and Reward model can be traced back to the Greek atomists, who drew a clear line between spirit and matter and believed in the dualism of body and soul. In the seventeenth century, the philosophy of René Descartes led to an extreme formulation of the spirit/ matter dualism. Descartes based his view of nature on a fundamental division into two separate and independent realms: that of mind and that of matter. This division has been beneficial for the development of modern science and technology but has had many adverse consequences for the development of our civilization. Descartes' famous sentence, *Cogito ergo sum* ("I think, therefore I am"), has led Western man to equate his

*Thomas Merton, *Raids on the Unspeakable.* New York: New Directions, 1964.

identity with his mind, and not with his whole being. As a consequence of this division, most individuals feel isolated "inside" their bodies. Thus separated, the mind was given the futile responsibility of controlling the body, creating a conflict between the two. This inner fragmentation mirrored the outside world, which was seen as a multitude of separate parts existing for the benefit of separate interest groups. The belief in the separateness of all these groups has alienated us from nature and other human beings.

In contrast to the mechanistic Western view, the Eastern view of the world stresses the ultimate unity of the universe. Although many variations exist among schools of Eastern mysticism, their basic teaching focuses on developing an awareness of the unity and mutual interrelation of all things, transcending the notion of an isolated individual self, and identifying oneself with the ultimate reality. The division of nature into separate objects is not fundamental and objects are considered to have a fluid and ever changing character, with time and change considered essential features.

It is interesting to see that twentieth-century science, which originated in the Cartesian split and mechanistic world view, is overcoming this fragmentation and returning to the early Greek and Eastern philosophies. This same phenomenon is being paralled by Western humanists and many of today's young people whose interest in the organic and ecological world view of the Eastern philosophies is due to disenchantment with a mechanistic, fragmented view. In this context, Virginia's view of the universe rides the crest of the new Western wave of those interested in exploring new ways to develop into healthy, joyous, and productive human beings with an appreciation for the miracle of being alive.

Virginia sees the goal of her work as one of helping people and families to gain a sense of their wholeness, wholeness being the fundamental characteristic of the universe. According to Gen. Jan Smuts (once prime minister of South Africa), who reintroduced holism into Western thinking, "This is a whole-making universe; it is the fundamental character of the universe to be active in the production of wholes, of ever more complete and advanced wholes," human personality being the consummation of this forward movement. All human beings strive toward holism or completion of themselves, although blockages can occur. The therapist's task is to help clients remove the blocks and barriers to this achievement.

Virginia believes in the Freudian adage that love and work are essential characteristics of the mentally healthy person. The ability to give and receive love is as important to the soul as inhaling and exhaling air is to the body. As to work, it represents an important source for one's feeling of self-worth. In addition, a mentally healthy person strives for a balance between physical, mental, emotional, and spiritual development and has a positive self-image. Such a person is willing to take risks leading to new possibilities, even if they are totally unfamiliar; does not seek to preserve the status quo; and is constantly engaged in a process of sorting out and letting go of what no longer fits, while adding new things that may fit. Such a person is willing to live with some ambiguity and tries to be nothing other than himself. Such a person is able to practice what Virginia has articulated as the Five Freedoms:

- "To see and hear what is here, instead of what should be, was, or will be.

- To say what one feels and thinks instead of what one should.
- To feel what one feels, instead of what one ought.
- To ask for what one wants, instead of always waiting for permission.
- To take risks in one's own behalf, instead of choosing to be only 'secure' and not rocking the boat."

How Individuals Grow and Develop

Three different types of factors influence the development of human beings. First are the unchangeable genetic endowments that determine an individual's physical, intellectual, emotional, and temperamental potential. This aspect will not be elaborated here. Second are longitudinal influences, which are the result of all the learning an individual acquires. Third are the constant interactions of body and mind.

Longitudinal Influences

At any moment, an individual's thoughts, feelings, and behaviors are determined by longitudinal influences: the sum of his learning experiences since birth. Although an individual is exposed to many different important types of learnings, the subsequent discussion focuses on those learnings that have to do with the development of self-identity and personhood.

A child enters the world in a situation of great inequality with those around him. At birth, he is completely helpless. His survival depends on the experiences, instructions, and behavior of his caretakers, usually his parents. Any adult, therefore, regardless of how deprived he feels his early childhood was, received some care as an infant, or he would not have survived. In addition to providing the food and love needed for his physical and emotional survival, his parents are also responsible for all the early learnings and images he forms about the world. The child learns from what he sees, hears, and understands. He develops an understanding of the world through his senses.

Since the nature of humans is to make sense of the world, the child makes up what he does not understand. Later, the conscious and unconscious memories of childhood become an interesting blend of truth and illusion. To the extent that communication is dysfunctional in a family, the child distorts information in his making-sense process. Later in life, this may affect his coping ability.

The first important consideration is that the foundations for adulthood, as well as the seeds for coping deficiencies, are formed in the family. Virginia views the experience of the primary triad (father, mother, and child) as the essential source of identity of the "self." On the basis of his learning experience in the primary triad, the child determines how he fits into the world and how much trust he can put in his relationships with other people. For instance, a child who in his first months of life experienced many feelings of abandonment is likely to have a difficult time forming close, intimate relationships with others unless new learnings can replace the early experiences. It is also in the primary triad that early in life the child develops coping mechanisms to deal with stress. Most stress patterns that individuals experience in their adult lives have their origin in the cradle. These stress patterns will be examined in chapter 3.

The primary triad also teaches the child about discrepancies in communication—inconsistencies between what he observes and what he is told, or between what he feels and hears—and where he first needs to interpret incongruent messages. The following example illustrates this point. The child, seeing his mother frown, asks, "What is wrong?" The mother, who has a rule that says "I must always be happy," responds, "Nothing, I am feeling just fine." Then she turns her back, probably in an effort to conceal from her child the intolerable conflict between what she feels she should be and what she is. The child may come up with many interpretations of the observed discrepancy, including the possibility that he may have some responsibility for his mother's unhappiness. Most parents are not aware of their incongruent messages. Some think they should shield their children from negative messages for fear that they might hurt them. Actually, negative messages, even if they are straight messages of rejection of the child, are less detrimental to the child's mental health than the mixed messages he is unable to figure out. Most of what children learn, and all they learn in the first months of life, is learned not from words but from voice tone, touch, and looks.

Another characteristic of the triad is that one person may feel excluded in certain situations. Indeed, most meaningful communications in the primary triad take place between two people at a time: mother–father, mother–child, or father–child. If the child feels excluded from interactions in the primary triad, perceives this exclusion as a rejection, and develops low self-worth as a result, he is setting himself up for a life of frustrations. He may feel that whenever he is not at the center of a triadic interaction, the two other members of the triad have something better going. A child who feels that he is usually excluded from interactions in the primary triad may easily develop feelings of low self-worth. A mother or father with low self-esteem could come to the same conclusion, but we are emphasizing the child since our focus here is on the development into adulthood.

The primary triad, then, is the first place where children learn about inclusion and exclusion and their place in the world. Unless modified by subsequent different learning experiences, these learnings will shape their personality.

By being part of a triad, the child also develops a sense of his own power. He may learn about manipulation as he becomes part of a potential coalition with either parent against the other. This process may manifest itself in early infancy, as in the case of a mother who feels that her husband is not handling the child properly. Although he is not aware of it at first, this gives the infant the power to affect the relationship between his parents, as his mother withdraws from the conjugal dyad to occupy herself in the relationship with her baby. Later on, such a child will learn how to use his power effectively to form a coalition with either parent, based on what seems for him a more advantageous outcome.

Virginia often uses the example of thumb sucking to illustrate the complexity of the interactions concerning one simple behavior and to show how the child may be affected by it.

Many small children enjoy sucking their thumbs. Let us pretend that the owner of this thumb is a child with a mother who has no objection to seeing her child suck his thumb and enjoys his contentment about it, so that each time the child sucks his thumb he feels the appreciation of his mother. This obviously will be a reinforcement for him. But the father says to himself, "Oh my God, the child is going to have terrible teeth." Right away, he feels he has got to get the thumb out of the child's mouth. So when the child is around his mother he feels reinforced, and when he is around his father he realizes that he should not suck his thumb. So far, no real conflict exists for the child. Children recognize early that different sets of expectations come from different people. The problem arises when the child sucks his thumb in the presence of both parents. Several scenarios are then possible, which will affect the picture of the world that the child develops.

The first scenario could be as follows. When the child sucks his thumb in front of both parents, the parents have agreed not to disagree because they are afraid they would hurt each other by disagreeing. So the issue of the thumb does not come up at all.

Another scenario is that the father looks at the child, sees the thumb, and tells the mother to do something about it. Now the thumb does something else: it can cause a fight if the mother asks why he doesn't do it himself. It sounds very much like father and mother are talking about the thumb, but they are actually talking about who has the right to tell whom what to do. At that moment, the parents can turn to the child and say, "You get us into trouble." This gives their son the awesome power to create considerable negativity between them.

In the third outcome possible, the triad operates with positive effect. The husband might share with his wife his concern that thumb sucking would lead to a lot of orthodontic work. His wife might answer that she was not aware of this and that she appreciates the comfort that the thumb gives the child. Then both the husband

and wife would be looking at other ways in which they could provide comfort or limit the thumb sucking. The point here is that the child would never be accused of interfering with his parents' relationship because of his thumb. In other words, the child does not get blamed. This situation also teaches the child that it is possible for people to build with one another instead of using their differences as weapons.

One additional point should be made here about triads. As one reviews the literature, one finds that the triad is frequently presented with negative connotations. This is evident in the title of Caplow's book, *Two Against One,* which implies confrontation, and in the writings of Bowen, who views the family of three as an interlocking and fluid system of dyadic coalitions that isolate the third individual at any given moment.

Indeed, the forces of the triad are powerful and often are in the hands of people struggling with the problems of their own survival and self-esteem. As a result, the outcome often appears negative. On the other hand, a triadic situation can be a source of strong support when three people agree to put their resources together and create a "basket" of possibilities from which they can draw as needed. In healthy families where self-esteem ranks high, the forces of cooperation are stronger than any temporary coalitions.

Most individuals and families who come into therapy do not function effectively in triadic relationships. One of the purposes of therapy is to restore the individual's ability to function effectively in a triadic setting. Parents need to realize the importance of good triadic relationships within their families. This certainly does not mean total agreement between parents (which is impossible unless one parent completely gives up his autonomy, which would bring about an entirely new set of problems), but that parents need to find an effective way to handle their differences. In the thumb-sucking example, it was the incongruency of the parents when they were together that created a problem, not the fact that they had different opinions about thumb sucking. In other words, the specific content of an experience does not generally have a bad effect, but the subliminal messages around the experience may.

We have dealt with the most simple expression of triadic life within the family by discussing a family in which there is only one child. As additional children are born the complexity of triadic formations increases geometrically, and so does the complexity of family interactions. The accompanying illustration shows how a family of more than three is made of sets of interlocking triangles (Bowen, 1972; and Caplow, 1968) that form what Virginia calls a can of worms.

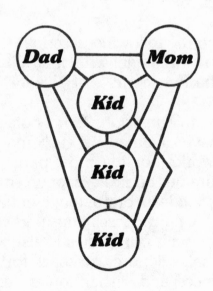

The Interplay of Mind and Body

Virginia sees the core of every person, the "self," as being in the center of a *mandala*. This graphic symbol consists of eight separate elements or levels which interact with one another and exert a constant influence on the well-being of the person.

"Listed, they are *physical* (the body); *intellectual* (the left brain, thoughts, facts); *emotional* (the right brain, feelings, intuition); *sensual* (the ears—sound, the eyes —sight, the nose—smell, the mouth—taste, and the skin—tactile-sensation-touch-movement); *interactional* (the I–Thou, communication between oneself and others, and communication between the self and the self); *nutritional* (the solids and fluids ingested); *contextual* (colors, sound, light, air, temperature, forms, movement, space, and time); and the *spiritual* (one's relationship to the meaning of life, the soul, spirit, life force)."

This quote and the following description of these eight levels is based on material written by Virginia as a contribution to the Festschrift for Salvador Minuchin.

"*The Physical Dimension.* Our bodies are miracles. Who could have dreamed up such marvels and then made them work? For the most part, we have been taught to ignore our bodies except when they are dirty, sick, too fat or too lean, or not the right height or shape. The idea of loving, appreciating, understanding, and communicating with our bodies is just beginning.

When one hates, ignores, or takes for granted one's body, imbalances and disharmonies result. This can show up in different manifestations affecting the body, and also the feelings, thoughts, and actions. Having these eight levels makes us a tapestry of parts, each part influencing and being influenced by others.

The Intellectual Dimension. Our intellectual part stems largely from the left brain, really the left hemisphere. It is the thinking part of ourselves. Here we draw conclusions, make rules, accept beliefs, and become scholarly. The left brain is a marvelous vehicle for processing factual data. When it acknowledges the right brain as an equal partner, it can create all kinds of excitement, discovery, and curiosity for its owner.

Unfortunately, Western culture has somehow given a much higher status to the activities of the left brain. In fields where knowledge and scholarship are uppermost —science, medicine, technology, etc.—the right brain has been downgraded, with a result that we are impoverished. Only people in the arts are esteemed for their right-brain work.

Historically, most women have been perceived as being incapable of rational, logical thinking. Men, on the other hand, have denied the value of their right brain and have often downgraded women for their emotions. This has made us a culture of "half-wits," and many disturbances in male–female relationships can be traced to this. This seems to be changing. We may be entering a period where we know that human beings have to have, acknowledge, and use both right and left brain, and to honor both our thinking and feeling parts so that we can become "whole-wits."

The Emotional Dimension. Recent findings suggest that the right brain (together with our nervous and glandular systems) is the main vehicle by which we monitor and experience our feelings. Feelings are the vehicle by which we experience life's happenings. They are the "juice" that gives color, texture, and tone to our lives. In the interest of being acceptable, human beings often ignore, deny, distort, or project their feelings. This, in turn, distorts their perceptions and inhibits their creativity and competence. All of this contributes to their state of poor-being. A further consequence is that people deny themselves the love and respect they so strongly desire from others.

Most of us in Western culture have been brought up to censor certain feelings such as anger, frustration, love (except with the "right" persons), and fear. The likely result is that we then ignore ("I didn't notice"), deny ("It didn't happen"), distort ("It is something else"), or project ("It is your fault") our feelings. Feelings are energy, and the energy does not go away just because feelings are not acknowledged. Instead, those feelings may take another form and resurface in destructive ways: physically, as in illness; intellectually, as in thought disturbances or limitations; or emotionally, as in nervousness or mental disorders.

The Sensual Dimension. We have beautiful sensory channels. Some people's channels do not work very well because their sensory organs are physically impaired. For people not so affected, sensory channels still might not work well. We can easily distort our perceptions to fit our expectations and/or past experience. Furthermore, our sensory channels have been affected by early admonitions of "don't look," "don't touch," "don't listen," and the like. As a result, our intake channels are working only part-time, and then only partially. In this situation, present conditions and people are not perceived as they really are. Instead, they are perceived as how they should be, how they were, or how they will be. This clearly can lead to imbalances.

The Interactional Dimension. Every human being came from two other people and was thus essentially born into a group. This probably accounts for what appears to be an inborn need to be in touch with other human beings. Because we were born little, we were in a life-and-death relationship with our parents, the Big Ones. As infants, we had no ability to survive on our own, and we had to put our survival in the hands of other people. We had, even as infants, needs greater than just physical care. We all had and have needs to be cared for, loved, and respected by others. This puts all of us in a vulnerable position with others, and it puts a tremendous burden on our links with other people. Our ongoing work in the world requires that we work with other people in capacities of trust and competence. When that does not happen, we are deprived of our need to achieve, and our self-worth is diminished. As described in the preceding section, disturbances, imbalances, and disharmony in our relationships with other people, especially family members, have a devastating effect on us. Relationship disturbances and negative inroads into self-esteem also result when feelings are systematically distorted. These imbalances reinforce the negative conditions, whether they are manifested on a personal or interactional level.

Until recently, these various levels have been treated as separate entities, and the care of each has resided with a specialist. Often these specialists had little or no understanding or appreciation of how that part was related to the other parts. Bodies were put in the hands of physicians, brains with educators, feelings with psychotherapists, souls with the clergy, and the rest in a no-man's-land.

In any given human being at any point in time, a dynamic interplay exists between all eight levels. It is as if there were a formula of A (body) + B (brain) + C (emotions) + D (senses) + E (interactions) + F (nutrition) + G (context) + H (soul) = S (self). All parts do add up to a self, although the self is more than the sum of the parts. The truth remains that each of us is a system. While we can study and talk about each part separately, they function together, just like any system. Just like a family."

Learning and Change

Let us now turn our attention to Virginia's beliefs about learning and change, paying special attention first to the way in which they relate to each other and to therapy, second to the process by which they occur.

Virginia's goal in life, for herself as well as for her students, patients, or others who consult her, is for people to develop those qualities which will help them to become more fully human, and to make in themselves the changes necessary to bring this about. People she encounters are at different stages towards these goals, ranging from the very needy, who subsist at survival level in several areas of their lives, to very evolved human beings who live at the cutting edge of growth, striving to develop their humanity to the fullest. Between these two extremes is a wide range of those who maintain themselves in a stable position but feel they could be more fully alive.

At one end of the spectrum, people will want to change in order to further their growth, while at the other they will seek change because of unbearable pain and despair. The specific approaches towards change in these two extreme cases will, of course, be different, and so will the emphasis, but the essence of the change process will remain the same. People will need to be in touch with their life force and be willing to take whatever risks are necessary for change to occur. The process of learning and change necessitates the willingness and ability to acquire new awareness at a cognitive, emotional level, as well as at a visionary and intentional level. When the integration of these awarenesses takes place, the person has changed by acquiring a new experience that questions the old, regardless of the original motivation for change.

Let us examine some characteristics of the processes of learning and change as they relate to human beings. If we accept as a given a person's genetic endowment, everything else a person is (feelings, thoughts, and behaviors) comes out of his learnings. Although memory often fails people when they try to remember conscious, factual data, it is amazingly reliable about emotional learnings, especially those survival learnings they acquired as children in their primary triad. If life in the primary triad was extremely stressful, those stress patterns learned in childhood will affect the person throughout his life, unless they are replaced by new learnings. This, of course, is a commonly held belief in the field of psychotherapy, but many therapists are more concerned about the "unlearning" than they are about the "learning." They tend to focus on the negative luggage a person carries and believe that the role of the therapist is to help the person unlearn so he can relearn. Virginia believes that there is no need to focus on the extinction of old learnings, because change will occur through the additive process of "transformation and atrophy." By focusing on a new way of doing things or of coping that is better than the old way, the person will start using the new way and the old way will die of disuse.

Another belief held by Virginia is that the process of learning is enhanced and maximized when the person feels supported and thus willing and able to take risks. This does not mean that learning will always be pleasant and that the learner will not know times of discouragement and despair. At times, the therapist or teacher may have to be extremely tough as he helps the person overcome his resistances to learning and change.

This belief is the logical consequence of the Seed Model. Indeed, if a child is not born evil, there is no need to thwart his original nature. In this respect, Virginia attaches herself to a long line of philosophers and educators who believe that if a child's or individual's curiosity is not blocked, the desire to learn will be there.

Finally, Virginia, always respectful and attentive to individual differences, believes that when people are exposed to new behavioral learnings, they need to take for themselves only that which fits for them, rejecting knowledge with which they are not comfortable. She believes that the learning process is essentially a discovery or, more accurately, a rediscovery by the learner of knowledge that is already in himself—knowledge that he does not know he has—and that the answers to questions are to be found within the individual who asks them. Indeed, the answer that one person or family finds may fit for them and not for anyone else. The role of the teacher or therapist, then, is to use strategic questions to help the student or client find his own answers. This process is similar to the Socratic or maieutic process of learning, in which the role of the teacher, similar to that of a midwife, is to help the student in birthing an idea which was inside him. People feel great excitement when they get in touch with something they knew all along but did not know they knew.

This chapter has established the conceptual framework of Virginia's therapeutic concepts. We first reviewed her philosophical view of man's place in the world and the conditions necessary for developing his full potential. We then looked at the way individuals grow and develop, both as a result of being part of a family and because of the constant interactions of body and mind. Finally, we focused on Virginia's views about learning and change. Now we are ready for the next step: discovering how these concepts influence Virginia as a therapist.

Chapter 2
Goals of Therapy

This chapter examines the goals of Virginia Satir when she sees a family in therapy, or when she works with any human system that seeks growth. It also looks at the effect of these goals on the diagnostic process.

Her goal of therapy is to enhance individuals' potential for becoming more fully evolved as human beings. In family therapy, her goal-and-art is to integrate the needs of each family member for independent growth with the integrity of the family system.

Families come into therapy because of a problem that causes them frustration, despair, and pain and with which they are unable to cope by themselves. Often, they are referred to the therapist by a third party (legal, medical) who sees the family as unable to solve the problem on its own.

Virginia's goal as a therapist is to enable the family to gain new hope and to help it reawaken old dreams or develop new ones. If individual members of a family do not sense from the beginning that life can be different, they will not find the positive energy necessary for change. By putting the emphasis on hope, people enter the process of therapy with a positive feeling, whereas a primary orientation on the problem or problems is perceived negatively and is depressing to the individuals in treatment as well as to the therapist.

Her second goal of the therapist is to strengthen and enhance the coping skills of individual family members by teaching them new ways of viewing and handling situations. Emphasis is on the process of coping rather than specific problems. Problems are encountered by everyone in the process of living and can be looked at as challenges for coping. As therapists, we do not usually see people who are coping effectively with their problems. Thus, it is easy to think of the problem, rather than the inability to cope with it, as the cause of the trouble. In Virginia's view, the problem is just an acknowledgment of an inability to cope. Indeed, another person in a similar situation who copes differently may not perceive it as a problem. In brief, the task of the therapist is to help each family member with his own coping so that he can decide to do the things that work for him.

The goals of awakening hopes and developing coping skills, then, reframe the process of people coming into therapy in a positive light. To quote Virginia:

"My hope is that every interview will result in a new window for each person to look through with the result of feeling better about himself or herself and gaining the ability to do things more creatively with other members of his or her family. This is really what I mean by saying that I am dealing with a coping process rather than a problem-solving process. . . . I am not trying to solve a specific problem such as should they get a divorce or should they have a baby. I am working to help people find a different kind of coping process. I do not see myself as wise enough to know what is the best thing for a person to do. Should the wife ask her mother-in-law to leave? Should she *demand* that she leave? Should the wife leave her husband if the mother-in-law doesn't leave? These kinds of questions are not mine to answer. My task is to help each person with his or her own coping so that he or she can decide to do the things that work for him or her."*

Another goal of her therapy is to make people aware that they have the ability to make choices—small choices as they interact with each other, larger choices as they make important decisions about the conduct of their lives. This goal ties into the preceding one, since a person's awareness and appreciation of choices contributes to his ability to feel competent and able to cope.

The focus on coping skills rather than on problem-solving affects the way in which Virginia looks at symptoms and establishes a diagnosis. For her, the diagnostic process consists of exploring the life of a person or of a family in order to understand the underlying dynamics which led to the problem or to the hurt. In this light a symptom can be seen as an effort to adapt and survive by people who perceive themselves as living in an alien, hostile, and toxic system.

Another way of looking at a person or family with symptoms is that they are starving for something. When people feel starved on any level and consider themselves without resources, they will grab at anything that promises nurturing. This can lead some people to kill, steal, mutilate themselves, assault others, or cheat in order to alleviate their pain or anxiety. For some people, meeting their starvation needs in these ways is inconceivable, so they resort to other methods—drugs, alcohol, physical or mental illness, for example—that can serve to disengage the hunger from their consciousness. In other situa-

---

*Virginia Satir, *Conjoint Family Therapy,* third edition. Palo Alto, CA: Science and Behavior Books, 1983.

tions, some people see themselves as so without resources and meaning that they resort to suicide.

Virginia elaborates:

"For me, the symptom is analagous to a warning light that appears on the dashboard of a car. The light, when lit, says the system required to run the car is in some form of depletion, disharmony, injury or impairment. One part or a combination of parts may be breaking down. If any one part breaks down, the whole system is affected. Just as in the family.

I see the family and the individual in the same way. My emphasis is on understanding the message of the light, and then on searching for ways that family members deplete, block, or injure themselves and each other. My treatment direction is to release and redirect that blocked up energy, which means that I deal with their self-esteem, communication, and rules for being human as these relate to the eight levels of self.

My emphasis now is on developing and releasing health on all its levels. When that is achieved, the symptom no longer is necessary and withers away from disuse. I find that family rules can be changed to human guides that can support human health, growth, happiness and love—guides that are flexible rather than rules that are rigid. This means a harmonious interplay between all levels within oneself and between self and other members of the family."

In conclusion, the goals of Virginia's therapy are to develop health rather than eradicate symptoms and to transform into useful purposes the energy bottled up in a person's or a family's demonstrated pathology. Virginia refers to this approach as the Human Validation

Process Model. These goals are based on the holistic principle of transformation and atrophy described in the first chapter, which states that if the process that led to the development of the symptom can be altered, then the symptom will disintegrate. If people are healthy, symptoms are not necessary. The process is additive, and there is no need to remove anything.

Entering a dark room is analogous: when the electricity is turned on, the darkness is gone. All that was done was to add the light, without removing anything. Virginia's metaphor in the Minuchin Festschrift further illustrates this point:

"Let us imagine a wheel with a hub at its center and spokes reaching out to a rim. The spokes represent the various parts of a person. The rim represents the boundaries of a person.

In a pathology-oriented approach, one starts with emphasis on the pathology/symptom, the hub, making it the center of one's attention. Thus, one selects out in an individual only that which is destructive and symptom-related. In a health-oriented approach, I see the hub as the potential health of the individual—present but untapped, covered over, and therefore out of reach to that person. In this frame of thinking, the symptom is an attempt to express that health even though the individual, by his beliefs and rules, blocks the manifestation of that health."

Situations occasionally arise in family therapy wherein the therapeutic goals for the family conflict with those of one or more individuals in that family. For instance, it may become clear that the needs of the family as a whole may best be served by a child or even a parent being removed from the family at least temporarily. This does not mean that therapy has failed but that the original goals of family integration are better served by such a step. As an example, a handicapped child's needs for special care or limits may be so destructive to the remaining members that the family's integrity becomes threatened. This example also points out the need for goal reassessment as therapy progresses. Ultimately, by integrating the integrity of the family system with each member's needs for independent growth, family therapy can achieve its overall goal of enhancing the individual's potential for becoming more fully evolved.

Chapter 3
Areas of
Assessment
and Intervention

When watching Virginia work, the artistry of her orchestration, the warmth of the human connections, and the unfolding of the people present are so powerful that it becomes difficult to realize that important gathering of data and observation of the family system is taking place at the same time. This chapter describes the issues that Virginia assesses in order to move the family system from a symptomatic base toward one of wellness.

Assessment and interventions in Virginia's approach to family therapy reflect the fact that a family is a system. That is, every part is related to the other parts in a way such that a change in one brings about a change in all the others. Indeed, in the family, everyone and everything impacts and is impacted by every other person, event, and thing. Thus, in assessing the family, it is important to understand the multiple stimuli and multiple effects at work within the given family system.

Two basic kinds of systems are the *open* and the *closed* systems. In a closed family system, information to and from the outside world is very limited, and reactions to situations occur in a circular and automatic manner that disregards any changes in the context. In an open family system, reactions and interactions are affected by changes in the context or by new information.

The words open and closed are used here to express extremes rather than absolute realities. No human system can exist without some interchange with the environment. Conversely, even an open family system at times reduces its exchanges with the outside world.

Closed systems in families seem to operate on a set of rigid, fixed rules that are applied to a given context regardless of how those rules fit. Although these rules are often out of date, conforming to them seems more important than the needs of the individual family members.

A closed system is dominated by power, neurotic dependency, obedience, deprivation, conformity, and guilt. It cannot allow any changes, for changes will upset the balance. This varies in degrees with different families, of couse, but for many people the security of what they know, even when it is uncomfortable, is less threatening than risking the perils of the unknown.

The result of closed systems is that their members are kept ignorant, limited, and ruled through fear, punishment, guilt, and dominance. They experience increasing doubts about their self-worth, as they need frequent reinforcement from the outside to feel good about themselves. Such a system has to break down over time because someone in the system comes to the end of his coping ability. When this happens, one or more persons may develop symptoms.

An open system features choice and flexibility. It even has the freedom to be closed for a while if that fits. Self-worth is primary, with each family member experiencing a sense of power or control over his own fate.

The key to a healthy and open system is the ability to change with a changing context and to acknowledge that fact. It also allows the full expression and acceptance of hopes, fears, loves, angers, frustrations, and mistakes. In other words, the full range of what we know as human beings can be present without threat and can be expressed honestly, without any fear of rejection or humiliation.

There are, of course, varying degrees of being open or closed, but families tend to lean one way or another. Virginia elaborates in the Minuchin Festschrift:

"All systems in families are for the protection and management of their members. In closed systems, because they are managed largely by fear, the resources are experienced as limited and finite. People in closed systems live in a hostile world where love is counted in dollars, conditions, power, and status. In open systems, managed by love and understanding, resources are seen as ever-present possibilities. People live in full humanness with confidence, humor, realness, and flexibility. Problems are treated as challenges to be coped with rather than as things to be defeated by. Part of that process is seeking help when it is needed.

So what happens when a member of a system has trouble? A bad boy or girl has never been born. Only persons with potentials are born. Something in that human being has to be denied, projected, ignored, or distorted for him or her to become some kind of bad, sick, stupid or crazy boy or girl, man or woman. How this happens is easy for me to explain, but more difficult to change.

A person is simply the outcome of all the transactions—both intentional and unconscious—that occurred between the child and himself/herself and the other family members, especially the adults, who have had in their hands the power over his or her psychological life and death from the time of conception until the present. Infants are a captive audience for the beliefs of their parents and the society of which they are a part.

Human beings seem willing to pay whatever price is necessary to feel loved, to belong, to make sense, and to feel as if they matter, even if the price exacted doesn't really accomplish that. The self is willing to adapt to almost anything to try to get those things. This makes it possible for closed systems to continue as long as they do."

Self-Esteem/Self-Worth

Based on her experience with thousands of families, Virginia focuses her attention on the following areas: the self-worth of the individual family members, the communication patterns within the family, and the family rules.

Self-worth or self-esteem is the value that a person attaches to himself, the love and respect he has for himself, independent of the way others see him. A person with low self-worth experiences a great anxiety and uncertainty about himself and is unduly concerned about what others think of him. This dependence on others cripples his life.

Low self-worth is different from feeling low. One may feel discouraged, sad, or despairing without having low self-worth. Feeling low, however, becomes low self-worth when a person experiences feelings of unworthiness but is unable or is afraid to acknowledge these feelings. In other words, low self-worth has to do with what the individual communicates to himself about such feelings and the need to conceal rather than acknowledge them.

Low self-esteem tends to be contagious within a family. Often a person with low self-esteem selects to marry another person with low self-esteem. Their relationship is based on a disregard of inner feelings, and any stress tends to augment their feelings of low self-esteem. Children growing up in that environment usually have low self-worth.

Virginia views positive self-worth as the foundation of individual and family mental health. An individual with high self-worth has high respect for all the aspects of life, which enables him to use his energy constructively for himself and for others. The reverse is also true: low self-esteem has always been one of the most destructive human elements in the world.

Most of the problems brought into therapy by individuals and families are ultimately connected with low self-esteem. For this reason, it is essential that the therapist assess the presenting problems in terms of self-worth. In addition, raising the self-esteem of individual family members is one of the essential foci for intervention.

A problem in itself has no meaning independent of how the concerned individuals feel about it. A father in a wheelchair may require adaptation on the part of other family members and some restriction of the family's activities, but it becomes a problem only if the father feels ashamed or less of a person because of it, or if his condition affects the way other family members feel about him or about themselves. Being in a wheelchair is not itself a family problem unless the family makes it one. The same is true of many other difficult situations that a family may face. Conversely, it is important to realize that low self-esteem in one or more family members contributes significantly to many family problems such as substance abuse, spouse battering, or delinquency. Thus, the same event may activate issues of self-worth in one person and not in another. The only universal aspect is that when, for whatever reason, a person's self-worth gets hooked, the experience is scary and raises the issue of psychological and/or physical survival. If the person is not aware of what is happening, he will defend himself against the feeling. Instead of acknowledging it, he will blame, placate, react in a super-reasonable or irrelevant manner, drink, run away, get sick, etc.

To explore the self-esteem of family members, the therapist uses his visual observational skills to watch how individual family members present themselves and communicate with one another nonverbally, and his auditory skills to listen for the content and process of oral communication. Clueing into the meaning of the presenting problem in terms of a person's self-worth requires much skill because most people have strong built-in mechanisms for hiding their areas of low self-worth from themselves and from others. Nonetheless, assessing the presenting problem in terms of its meaning to individuals in the family is essential because trying to work only at the problematic or defense level does not deal with the key issue.

Communication Patterns

The second basic component of family functioning is communication. By assessing the general patterns of communication in the family, the therapist gains information about the way in which family members experience their relationships with one another, their ability to express intimacy, how they pass information back and forth, what meaning they make of their communication, and in general the ability of family members to use words appropriately. Since good communication is such an important factor in healthy family life, modification of the family's communication process is an essential focus of therapy. People usually intend to communicate well but often lack the tools to do so.

Functional communication exists when the speaker clearly and directly states or requests something, when both speaker and receiver can clarify and qualify what they say, and when feedback is possible. In good communication, the intent and the outcome of the communication match; or, if they do not, clarification is possible.

In a dysfunctional family, communications are indirect, unclear, and seldom clarified. When dysfunctional communicators relate an experience, they are likely to make statements that are incomplete, distorted, or inappropriately generalized. The family therapist needs to intervene by questioning the deletions, inaccuracies, and inappropriate generalizations (see Part I, comment 98). Helping family members become aware of their dysfunctional communications and teaching them more accurate patterns of communication make it possible to modify painful internal representations.

In *nominalization,* another dysfunctional communication process, active portions of an experience are represented by static words. Rather than saying "I am confused," for example, the speaker talks about "experiencing confusion." This changes the process of being (a verb) confused into a static event (a noun). By helping the communicator to *denominalize,* the therapist helps him rediscover and experience the feelings of movement and flow, which are essential to give the person the feeling that change is possible.

In the third dysfunctional process, called *complex-equivalence,* an individual equates one segment of someone's behavior with a total communication and then labels it as his own inner experience. For instance, when one family member frowns, another family member attends to the frown and ignores other behaviors and words that communicate additional information (see Casey's interpretation of the smirk on Margie's face, between comments 108 and 109). Or when one person looks away, the other assumes that he is not paying attention and feels hurt (comment 91).

Differences in major representational systems can also result in miscommunication. Bandler and Grinder wrote that an experience can be represented through three sensory channels: audition, vision, and kinesthesis. Most people tend to favor and use one of these channels more than the others. In the mind-reading example above, the person looking away may well be an auditory type for whom eye contact is actually a deterrent to concentration, while the receiver may be a visual person who cannot communicate without making eye contact. The therapist, by making family members aware of their differences in this respect, can help family members understand each other's idiosyncrasies in a positive light.

Finally, the way the family handles its communication reflects the self-worth of family members and thus provides additional information about the disharmony and dysfunction in the family system. In a family where low self-esteem is an endemic problem, the fear of exposing areas of vulnerability or of experiencing a loss of love prevents clear communication about feelings or intimate issues. The primary objective of communication becomes validation from other people. A person experiencing low self-worth is concerned with emotional survival, so his main concern when communicating with other people is his fear of revealing himself. When he uses communication to conceal and protect, there is a lack of congruence between his feelings and his behavior.

In her book *Peoplemaking,* Virginia describes four incongruent, or dysfunctional, communication stances: placating, blaming, being super-reasonable, and being irrelevant. These are different ways to hide the reality of one's feelings from oneself and from others. The placator hides his vulnerability by attempting to please others, saying yes not because he feels it but because his emotional survival depends on it. He feels that he is no good, but by doing what is expected of him, at least he will not be rejected. The blamer hides his vulnerability by attempting to control others and by disagreeing indiscriminately, thus giving himself a sense of his importance despite his inner feelings of loneliness and failure. For the super-reasonable person, every aspect of living becomes an intellectual experience that bypasses the inner self and ensures the anesthesia of any feelings. Everything becomes an "it." Although this posture conveys uninvolvement and control, the internal feeling is one of vulnerability. Finally, the irrelevant stance handles stress by pretending that it is not there. The person focuses elsewhere, away from the present context and away from feelings. Internally, the irrelevant person feels uncared for and alienated.

Most people are able to respond in any or all of these stances, although they usually have a preferred mode. An individual who chronically responds in the same manner may develop physical symptoms. The placator is likely to be affected in his digestive system; the blamer in his tissues and muscles; the super-reasonable person in the fluids of his body; and the irrelevant person in his central nervous system.

Interactions between people in these stances have a systemic aspect: none of the stances can survive without the support of another. A beautiful example of this point is the stress ballet of Margie and Casey. It is also important to realize that these survival responses are not part of one's genetic endowment. They are learned responses that started at the cradle in the primary triad, when the infant was indeed entirely dependent on his parents for his survival.

An assessment of these stances and of the family's manner of communicating provides guidelines for the therapist's intervention. To help the family communicate with congruence, the family therapist encourages individual family members to acknowledge their feelings and thoughts, respect them as belonging to them, and then choose how to express them. Both the placator and the blamer need help to realize how they cripple themselves by making their self-worth dependent on what other people feel and think about them. The super-reasonable person usually presents the biggest challenge because he is so shielded from his feelings that he needs an infusion of feelings through experiencing his life force. The irrelevant responder needs to learn to focus on the reality of his own feelings, those of others, and on the context of any given situation.

Virginia does not view the communication stances as rigid and unchangeable. Each of them can be "renovated" through the process of transformation and atrophy. When a person responds by placating, for instance, one of the ravages going on within him is that he keeps giving himself messages that he does not count for very much without others' approval. Once he knows how, he can transform his wish to please others into an ability to be tender and compassionate. He can become aware of his ability to make choices instead of just experiencing the automatic response that he always has to please everyone.

Similarly, transformed blaming becomes the ability to be assertive, to stand up for oneself. Everyone needs to be able to do this, but it must be done realistically rather than automatically. Renovated super-reasonableness becomes the creative use of intelligence. Using one's intelligence is delightful, but it becomes isolating and boring if it is used only to protect oneself. Renovated irrelevance becomes the ability to be spontaneous and to have fun.

Incongruence manifests itself by a discrepancy between the verbal and the nonverbal message. The therapist needs to monitor closely the subtle external modalities such as changes in voice tone, skin coloration, respiration, facial expression, posture, and gesture. If any of these seem misaligned, the therapist asks for clarification and thus furthers the therapeutic process by helping the person get in touch with feelings of which he is not aware.

In short, most families who communicate congruently are able to cope with problems as they arise. If they need help around a specific issue, they are able to obtain it without needing a major overhaul. Conversely, most families in therapy have communication problems that play a significant role in the dysfunction that led them to seek help.

Family Rules

Another important feature of the family system is the rules that govern the behavior of individual family members. Family rules encompass all the behaviors that family members believe should or should not be performed in a given situation. They include the overt rules—such as bedtime, curfews, and household responsibilities—as well as covert, unspoken rules of which everyone in the family is aware but never mentions—such as never speaking about father's drinking and never referring to mother's first husband or to the oldest son, who drowned when he was four. In her assessment of the family, Virginia explores a number of different rules that apply to the family system. Questions about and a description of some of the most important rules follow.

Are the rules humanly possible? A family in which no negativity ever emerges and in which everyone is expected to look happy at all times is attempting to live by an inhuman rule. Since it is impossible to be happy always, regardless of what happens, such a rule leads to concealment of feelings, isolation, and lack of intimacy. In addition, a person living by this rule may feel guilty whenever he is not happy, since he is disobeying. Feeling negative about one's feelings further contributes to low self-worth.

Are the rules up to date and relevant to a changing situation? This is an extremely important area in Virginia's eyes. For instance, is a fifteen-year-old boy expected to live by the same rules as his nine-year-old brother?

In a healthy family, change is usually welcomed, or at least considered an inevitable part of life. The family accepts continuous adjustments as family members move through the life cycle and encounter various vicissitudes of living. There is a basic faith that, even when the changes are not positive, better times lie ahead. In the dysfunctional family, on the other hand, change is usually threatening, and preserving the status quo becomes a major preoccupation.

What are the rules governing differentness? Some families value differences. Others consider them unacceptable and a source of trouble, creating increasing disruption as the children grow older. When differences are not welcomed, there are essentially two ways of dealing with them. The first is to pretend that they do not exist. In a marital pair, one of the partners will sometimes abandon his view on one subject and adopt that of his partner because it is easier than arguing. The second approach is to freely express one's objections to another's differentness. Dealing with differences in either of these ways can create severe disturbances in family harmony.

What rules surround the sharing of information? In some families, only parents share important information. Other families share information in such a way that it is incomplete, distorted, or misunderstood, resulting in many problems for family members. In such families, it is often not permissible to question what one does not understand, which in turn leads to some of the communication dysfunction described earlier.

A family often has areas of secrets intended to protect some family members—usually the children—from the reality of the world around them. Family members do not comment about these areas openly and often justify their secrecy with statements such as "You are too young to understand" or "What you don't know won't hurt you." These secrets are often intended to keep a good parental image, so that children will not know that mother had an abortion before she married, or that father has a drinking problem. (It helps when the children are totally unobservant.) Even when one is aware of family secrets, one does not talk about them. One treats them as if they did not exist.

What rules govern what family members can say about what they are feeling, seeing, and hearing? Can experiences be expressed to any family member, or are the emotional rules for parents different than they are for the children? When people in a family are not free to express what they have on their minds, their perceptions and feelings can go underground and create difficulties in the long run. Some families permit the expression of feelings if the feelings are deemed suitable ("You should/should not feel that way") or age and sex appropriate ("Boys don't cry when they are nine, only babies do"). This denies the validity of the person's experience. Some families allow themselves to express only positive feelings. Negative feelings should be denied and definitely should not be expressed for fear of rejection, ridicule, or of hurting another person (see comment 51).

Of special interest to the family therapist are the family rules regulating the display of affection and anger. Regarding the expression of affection, there are essentially two types of families: those that are openly affectionate and those whose family members do not express feelings and appear cold or indifferent towards one

another. There are many variations on these two basic
themes. In some families, for instance, husbands and
wives never express affection to each other in front of
their children. In others, fathers stop hugging their boys
when they reach a certain age (they have to grow up as
strong men and affection between males could be
viewed as homosexual). Similar inhibitions are applied
to daughters at or shortly after puberty. This sad state
of affairs is due to the confusion people often feel about
expressing affection versus taboos about sex.

Rules regulating the expression of anger are also very
significant. Some families frown on expressing anger
and view it as dangerous. Others consider the expression of anger appropriate in some situations and not
others, or appropriate between some family members
and not others. Finally, some families seem to be in a
constant state of eruptive anger. In families who express
little affection, children tend to behave angrily towards
one another, both physically and verbally. Indeed, the
need for contact is so strong that if it cannot be manifested in a positive manner, it will come out distorted as
anger and fighting. The family described in Part I is a
good illustration of this.

The therapist can intervene in the area of rules in
several ways. When rules are unclear and misunderstood, the problem is one of poor communication. Family members need help with their communication skills
at many different levels. In addition to making them
aware of their difficulties and giving them an opportunity to practice new forms of communication, the family
therapist's role is also to educate the family about their
dysfunction. As pointed out earlier, dysfunctional communication occurs for many reasons, one of them being
ignorance of more effective ways to communicate. The

educational role of the therapist is also called on to help families when their rules are outdated, unfair, unclear, inappropriate, or do not fit the present situation. The therapist helps the family assess and question the validity of their rules and helps them reject those rules that contribute to dysfunction in the family.

Very skillful intervention is required with rules whose main function is to protect one or several of the family members' self-esteem. These rules usually operate without people's awareness and can be touched on only when family members feel very secure with the therapist. Usually, as the self-esteem of individual family members increases, it becomes possible for them to let go of the protection provided by rules. This kind of intervention is often the focus of Stage 2 of therapy, which is described in the next chapter.

In conclusion, the role of the therapist is to help the family become aware of and reshape those rules that interfere with the harmonious development of their family life. When this occurs, a climate is created which allows communication to improve, and the self-esteem of family members can increase.

Chapter 4
The Human Validation Process Model

This chapter examines the process Virginia follows when she works with a family and what she models for those who want to study and practice her approach. Although the process described here focuses on family therapy, the same basic process applies to any other human system seeking change.

Virginia refers to her therapeutic approach as the Human Validation Process Model:

"At this time, I see that my therapeutic task lies in reshaping and transforming into useful purposes the energy bottled up in a person's or a family's demonstrated pathology. This is in contrast to my earlier belief that my task was limited to exterminating the pathology. I refer to my present approach as a health-oriented approach, although it is really more than that. I call it the Human Validation Process Model."

This model is the logical outcome of Virginia's beliefs about the process of change. Her first key assumption is based on a deep bone feeling that people are geared toward growth and change and are capable of all kinds of transformation. In this light, she views a symptom as an indication that impaired communication or the rules of the family are blocking the freedom of one or more members to grow. These rules are derived from the way in which parents attempt to maintain their self-esteem. They also provide the context within which children grow and develop their self-esteem. Since the self-esteem of individual family members has such a profound impact on the family system, helping individual family members to feel better about themselves is a major focus of the Satir approach to family therapy.

Her second assumption is that all human beings carry with them all the resources they need to flourish. The therapeutic process consists of helping people gain access to and learn how to use their own resources, thus giving them new coping skills. In this context, the symptom is only a starting point, an explanation of how people cope at present. The therapist needs to understand what the symptom is, since it gives the clues to the malfunction, but the focus of therapy is on the process that brought about the malfunction.

Virginia's third assumption is that the family is a system wherein everyone and everything is impacted by and impacts everyone and everything else. Any situation is thus the result of multiple stimuli and multiple effects, which in turn means that blame cannot be assigned to individuals. The task of the therapist is to make this fundamental system concept alive for the family.

Fourth, Virginia assumes that the person and beliefs of the therapist are the most important tools at his command. To help people change by following this approach, he must believe that human beings are capable of growth and change, that they have in themselves the resources they need, and that problems are multicausal. He must also be able to model for family members the quality of congruence, which they need to develop in order to change. His ability to respond to the underlying messages of what is being communicated and the nonjudgmental qualities of his responses are essential: they provide new models of communication to the family. The humanness of the therapist is more important than his expertise.

These four assumptions underlie a process of therapy that is not easy to observe. When watching Virginia work, one is confronted with an overwhelming amount of information: the way she moves, her voice tone, the way she touches, who she turns to next, the sensory cues she uses to orient herself to different members of the family, etc. It is easy to lose the forest for the trees and difficult to see her very systematic approach and organization. The process usually flows smoothly, without any apparent transitions, and hides the fact that Virginia is highly structured about her process.

The Human Validation Process can be divided into three stages. They are not always easy to isolate since they do overlap, but they have distinct characteristics. Each phase is usually manifest in each session, although different phases may vary in length. They also characterize the overall movement of the therapy.

The first stage consists of establishing contact and making an informal working contract. The second stage is characterized by chaos, during which the therapist intervenes in the family system and disturbs the status quo. The third stage consists of a new integration.

Stage 1: Making Contact

The first stage, Making Contact, starts when the therapist meets with the family and ends when the therapist thinks he has gathered enough information and established enough trust to move into the next stage.

Families usually come into therapy on the basis of something negative. They may feel pain and helplessness about one or several problems and often have some feelings of shame. They are usually anxious about what might happen. The first task of the therapist is to make them comfortable and create a feeling of hope and trust, which will enable family members eventually to take the risks necessary for change to occur. To do this, the therapist takes an active role in creating the environment and directing the therapy. Displaying direction, knowledge, and comfort in his role of therapist communicates his lack of fear and his ability to handle painful material.

At the very beginning, Virginia makes a human connection with everyone, often in the form of a handshake. Devoting full attention to the person she is engaging gives him a sense that at that moment he is the only person who counts. It is essential that every family member be engaged and validated in such a manner, since often (especially in a dysfunctional family) at least one family member feels that he does not count for much in the family. Every family member must have a sense of being a unique individual in the eyes of the therapist. An excellent example of individualizing a family member occurs in comment 6, when Virginia asks the twins for suggestions on how to tell them apart. The simple process of making a human connection and listening to each person with genuine interest raises the self-esteem level of individual family members, making them feel better about themselves and making them hopeful that better things may be possible.

Another way to foster trust is to create a safe climate in which family members do not worry about the consequences of revealing something about themselves or other family members. Thus, it is important for the therapist to be absolutely nonjudgmental when responding to a description of events that might bring out a negative reaction in a nontherapeutic situation. Virginia's response in comment 11, when she tells Coby that angry responses can happen sometimes, provides a good illustration of this point. Family members also realize that the therapist believes all feelings are legitimate when the therapist's responses indicate that other people have similar feelings (comments 20 and 22).

Creating an informal atmosphere in which individual family members do not feel intimidated and realize that they can behave in a natural manner also develops trust. Virginia often adds to the informality by using personal examples that tell family members that she too has human concerns and that she will draw from her own experience when necessary. In comment 4, for instance, she lets Lucy and Lisa know that she has twin brothers. In comment 10, she makes a bridge with Coby by relating an incident of her childhood.

During this initial phase, when little seems to be happening on the surface, the important task of teaching individual members new skills and helping them use their existing skills has already started. Family members are helped to pay better attention to what they see (comment 14) and to report their observations in a nonjudgmental manner. By learning to become more fully aware of what is going on inside themselves (feeling) or outside themselves (seeing, hearing, touching), family members can relate to each other as they are in the present situation instead of relying on past memories and on their imaginations.

At this point, a superficial observer might wonder when the session will really start. Indeed, five to forty-five minutes or more may go by before Virginia establishes the reason for the family visit. This is due to Virginia's belief that the therapist needs to gain acceptance by family members before he can explain his view of the situation in a meaningful manner.

During this informal opening process, while family members are developing trust within the therapeutic situation, Virginia is gathering essential information for the conduct of the session. Although she may not fully know the reason the family is seeking help, she is gaining an initial understanding of the family system and developing some hypothesis about the way the family copes with many aspects of living. By the way family members talk about themselves, she learns how they feel about themselves. By the way they talk to each other, she learns whether they tend to support or denigrate each other's self-worth and the kind of communication problems that this family may have. She also gathers information about some of the rules governing the family system. By focusing on the communications and on the self-worth issues that emerge, she gains an understanding of the survival skills or defenses used by individual members to protect their self-esteem. She needs this information to help individual family members change and grow.

In Virginia's approach to therapy, gathering information about the process of family life, or the family system, is essential. Changing those processes is the focus of therapy, while the problem itself takes a back seat and is seen only as a consequence of a dysfunction in the family system.

Having thus established contact and begun to gather information about the family system, Virginia then turns her attention to what brings the family into therapy. She asks about hopes, change, or expectations rather than "problems" (comment 17). She may ask each family member in turn. Sometimes, as with the family in Part I, she may ask only one or two family members if she senses that other family members agree with what has been stated. The slow pace that characterized the beginning of this stage usually begins to pay off now, as family members begin to show their willingness to deal with meaningful issues.

Virginia starts her interventions in the family system before she completes her assessment. This overlap benefits both the family and the therapist. The family develops a sense of the possibility of change and gets actively engaged in the intervention, while the therapist has an opportunity to assess the family further.

The interventions made in the first stage have distinct characteristics. Virginia's major therapeutic goal in this initial stage is to make manifest for family members what she has observed and to make explicit what family members often know implicitly. (This happens in comment 28, when Virginia remarks that there are short fuses in this family.) She does not act on the content of her observations but simply states that "this is the way I see things," without attaching any judgment to the statement. First-stage interventions may also make family members aware that different people have different

pictures of the same situation. This awareness is important for their understanding of their own family system
and family dynamics.

Virginia often brings to life what she sees happening
by involving family members experientially and having
them act out or "sculpt" the situation (comments 38, 40,
and 41). Although sculpture is not the exclusive domain
of stage 1, it seems appropriate to mention it here,
because it provides so much diagnostic information
about the family. Using sculpture involves several or all
family members and can clarify a situation much faster
than if individual family members share their perceptions verbally. In addition, the sculpting process is dynamic, brings out new information and awareness, and
is often humorous (at least in part). The family's ability
to laugh at what is going on is often a major therapeutic
step.

During this first stage, Virginia asks family members
a number of questions about their feelings. She takes
care to do this at a comfortable level: she does not probe
beyond defenses, and people express only those feelings that are already in the family's public domain.

Often, many family members express angry feelings
in the early phase of the interview. On the surface, this
might appear to be one of the key dynamics in this
family. It is important to note that Virginia does not
dwell or focus on the anger, although she is very aware
of its presence. She often chooses to bypass it for the
time being because she believes that focusing on the
anger without having developed some positive contact
will open up a bottomless pit. Her view is that people
use anger defensively to cover up feelings of hurt, pain,
despair, fear, isolation, and the like. People hide their
feelings behind anger to protect their self-esteem (com-

ment 78). Virginia's approach is to prepare an atmosphere in which she can help family members deal directly with their underlying emotions. If she perceives
that anger is creating a severe problem in the family, she
may help family members find a more creative way of
handling their angry feelings, which is different from
making anger the focus of the therapy.

During this stage, the therapist also assesses the
boundaries of each family member. Physically and emotionally, how close can he get with each person? To
know how much risk to take during the second stage of
the interview, the therapist must take into account each
member's fears and needs.

In this initial phase of therapy, many therapists like to
develop a working contract with the family. They dis-
cuss mutual expectations, the length and number of
sessions, and other important details of the therapeutic
relationship. Virginia negotiates such a contract when it
seems appropriate, but her approach is marked by such
flexibility that she does not usually know at this stage
where working with this family might lead her. However, she does establish an informal contract based on
trust, in which she lets family members know that they
remain in control of the decision about how much risk
they are willing to take, and that she will not push them
to cross boundaries for which they are not ready.

Stage 2: Chaos

The second stage of the therapeutic process is very accurately labeled as Chaos. Whereas the status quo was maintained in the first stage, the second stage is characterized by general confusion and disorder. Virginia helps one family member or more to go beyond the protected and defended areas to those areas he is afraid to reveal either to himself or to others. This is when the lid on anger is lifted and the person is enabled to express his underlying pain, vulnerabilities, and the frailties of which he is ashamed. While expressing this hurt and pain creates a considerable amount of anguish, it is the sine qua non for creating intimacy and a supportive climate in the family.

This chaos phase is characterized by the willingness of one or more family members to risk moving into unknown territory. The person experiencing the risk has a feeling of impending doom as he is flooded by irrational fears. Those fears are similar to those experienced in early infancy when the removal of love was synonymous to death and when his extreme dependency on others for survival meant that he was completely vulnerable. This same fear is present, at some level, in any person who moves into the unknown. The risk is usually purely psychological, although physical symptoms, if present in a family member, can sometimes become manifest. For example, an asthmatic attack could be precipitated, as could an epileptic seizure (this was the case with the identified patient depicted in the film *A Family in Crisis**).

The first time a person experiences the agony of mov-

*Virginia Satir, *A Family in Crisis.* Palo Alto: Science and Behavior Books, 1972.

ing into the unknown is the most frightening. At that moment, he is not able to count on his own resources and jumps without knowing where he will land. In the course of therapy, this life-and-death apprehension gradually loses its intensity as successive resolutions enable the person to live with the ambiguous feeling of uncertainty. The individual is also able to associate this feeling with his ensuing mastery and growth in new areas.

When someone takes a risk and reveals himself, the content of his revelation is usually frightening only to himself. The breakthrough is not in the content of what he says but in the fact that he has been willing and able to share something that had been unspeakable for him. This is the first step a person takes to get to his core. The process of allowing oneself to move into vulnerable areas heralds one's willingness to make fundamental changes.

The interventions at this stage, while not markedly different from what they are at other stages of the therapy, have special characteristics which contribute to the uniqueness of this second stage. The therapist must be clear, tough, and forceful in helping the person through this impasse. The toughness in Virginia (comments 47 and 52) is always present when needed, although sometimes hard to detect because her style is still to be caring and gentle in her toughness. She manifests toughness in relation to the person's obstructive part only after she has established a therapeutic alliance with him. In other words, she has allied herself with the individual's growth goal and has teamed up with the parts of that person desiring growth. If this therapeutic alliance is not present, Virginia will not push because she would then be violating the person's defended territory and trust. Until the person is willing to take the risk, growth cannot occur. If trust and the willingness to change are not present, the forcefulness of a therapist is analogous to force-feeding, and the resistance to it prevents genuine change.

Observers sometimes marvel at the ease with which Virginia obtains cooperation from family members and attribute this cooperation to Virginia's charisma. Although this may be present, the chief reason she obtains cooperation is that she is in tune with which risks family members are willing to assume at a given moment and gives them the support they need to overcome their impasses (comments 79–84).

In addition to supporting the person she works with, Virginia supports other family members at the same time. She maintains contact with what is happening with other family members and shifts her attention to an emergent issue when necessary (comment 62). If a therapist neglects an emergent issue and proceeds as if he had not heard, the family may assume that he is unable to handle the present situation.

Another important point in the chaos stage is that the therapist needs to keep the client focused towards the present. People in this phase are in touch with their inner turmoil more than with the reality around them, and their fears are reinforced by memories of the past or uncertainties about the future (comment 101). The task of the therapist is to bring them into the present, helping them use their senses and forcing them to pay attention to what is real rather than what is imagined. A good example occurs in comment 90, when Virginia brings Margie back into the present by asking her to feel Casey's skin through her hands. The emphasis is on the present as the only reality; as the client becomes more comfortable with this reality, he can regain a sense of mastery over his destiny. Make no decisions at this stage that cannot be carried out in the next ten to fifteen seconds.

The artistry of Virginia's therapy is evident in the balance she achieves between toughness and empathy. She has infinite patience as she tries to find another channel and another bridge. Such mastery is hard to achieve. Because of the turmoil and skills involved, some therapists stay away from this stage, which is absolutely essential for change to occur.

Having discussed the risks taken by family members, we must point out that the feeling of risk is not any less for the therapist. During the stage of chaos, he must have many skills at his immediate command, not knowing in advance which one to use. He must make rapid decisions and accept the ambiguity of not knowing where he is going. The severity of the reactions he may encounter are unknown. In addition, the therapist is open to the same vulnerabilities as any other human being, including rejection by the client if the therapist has overestimated the strength of their relationship or the client's ability to accept support (comment 70).

Stage 3: Integration

The third stage, Integration, occurs when closure has been made on the issue that created the turmoil in the preceding stage. Whereas the second stage is characterized by feelings of stuckness, hopelessness, and an inability to move backward or forward, the third stage is characterized by hopefulness and a willingness to do things in a new way. Of variable length, this stage is a time of emotional rest, enabling the family to work through an issue with the therapist if necessary. Integration can mark the end of the session or just be the punctuation necessary before the cycle starts again. If the session does not end after the third stage, a smooth transition is possible between the closure of one issue to the opening of a new one. Obviously, the Making Contact stage will not need to be as elaborate in subsequent cycles as when the family and the therapist were getting acquainted.

The stages of therapy are not as clearly delineated in practice as in the description above. They often overlap, and all family members are usually not in the same stage at the same time. In Part I, for instance, both parents move into stage two when Virginia is working with them exclusively, while the children do not share the full extent of their parents' anguish (with the exception of Lisa, comments 62–63).

It is essential that the therapist know which stage of therapy is in progress. Of special importance is that the session not end before the family has had an opportunity to integrate what happened during the phase of chaos. This is especially crucial in the first interview, and if the therapist has only a limited time available, he should wait until the following session before moving into the second stage.

Another way of looking at these three stages is as a cyclical movement occurring in therapy. The first cycle represents a hologram of the whole treatment. In the interview in this book, the cycle is reproduced only once (stage two starts when Margie is able to get in touch with what she wants and takes the risk to ask for it). Stage three ends when Margie and Casey sit down after the stress ballet and are able to work out an agreement for an outing.

In therapy, Virginia views herself as the leader of the process, meaning that her expertise is in helping people to make decisions about their lives and not in making decisions for them. The distinction between being a leader of the process and being a leader of the people is important: a therapist can lead people only if they relinquish control of the decisions about their lives, in which case no therapy is taking place. Virginia very carefully checks out with the people involved their willingness to participate in new experiences, and she makes them aware of the risks involved. This keeps participants in charge of their lives and assures the therapist of their understanding, trust, and willingness to take risks (comment 109).

As leader of the process, the therapist also sets the tempo of the session. At times the interview seems to progress very slowly, at others by fast leaps.

Virginia's focus on process is not always apparent. At times, she spends a long period on specific situations which might lead one to believe she is very content-oriented. The content under examination, however, usually has little to do with what the family perceives as a problem. Instead, it gives family members an opportunity to work through an issue about which they do not feel defensive, and it allows the therapist to observe interactions of family members at many levels. A good example of this is at the beginning of Part I when Virginia finds out from family members how they tell the twins apart. Specific details like this help the therapist form a picture of family processes. Family members who learn problem-solving skills on one issue can then transfer those newly acquired skills to other situations (comment 98).

In process therapy, the overall direction of treatment often takes a back seat to an emergent need. The art of therapy is in maintaining a balance between the overall direction of the therapy and new issues that emerge along the way. The process can be compared to threading a needle: if one ignores the small knot that has formed by the eye of the needle, the threading gets blocked. Similarly, the therapist who neglects to deal with a frown or other seemingly unimportant detail runs the risk of creating a blockage in the process. Virginia checks her interventions every step of the way to make sure that no knot has formed (comment 88).

Virginia often compares her therapy to weaving. The process of weaving consists of picking up strands that often appear unrelated and connecting them until they eventually form a coherent design. Similarly, one thought, or strand, expressed by a family member is expanded by using other family members' input. Then another strand is picked up and developed. A strand that had been dropped is later picked up again. Eventually, the seemingly disconnected strands combine to form a new design.

Finally, a comment needs to be made about the way in which a therapeutic session with Virginia is rich in cognitive information. As stated earlier, Virginia makes little distinction between teaching and therapy, which she views as part of the same continuum. After years of experience as a family therapist, she sees problems that she once would have considered emotional in nature as being the result of an educational lack. As an example, most people in our culture have never been encouraged to see properly. As a result of an educational process that starts in infancy, children become aware that there are many things they should not see, or at least not comment on. Looking at people for any length of time is considered especially rude, so we are conditioned to pay attention to our own images rather than to the reality out there. For similar reasons, people who do not pay attention to their internal messages need to be specially prompted to pay attention to their feelings. In short, peoples' ability to practice what Virginia calls the Five Freedoms is largely hampered by an educational lack. It is present not only in the families seen in therapy, but in most therapists as well.

For this reason, the processes used in the training of family therapists are very similar to those used in therapy. The interview contains many examples of Virginia using a teaching mode (comments 8, 29, 42, 59, and 69).

Chapter 5
The Family
Therapist as
a Person and
a Professional

There are different ways of relating to the way Virginia works. Some people, after watching her, have rushed out and used her techniques in a "cookie cutter" approach without understanding the context in which she uses her tools. Others are so awed by what they see that they consider her a unique phenomenon, isolating her as some kind of guru with special magical skills that common mortals do not possess. Without taking anything from the special artistry with which Virginia works and her very special ability to draw people to her, it is important to stress that such an attitude does not recognize the tremendous amount of effort and work she devotes to the development of her skills. What usually is referred to as intuition, even granting some innate ability, is the result of many years of learning and appreciating human and family processes.

Between these two extremes is another category. Impressed by Virginia's approach, some people have learned and integrated many of her approaches into the unique way in which they work. Usually, those who become her serious students have been attracted by her work because it strikes a responsive cord in them.

The preceding chapter focused on the process Virginia follows when she works with a family. This chapter focuses on the qualities that a therapist wanting to use this approach needs on both a human and professional level. Addressed first is the need to be committed to the assumptions and values that underlie the Satir process, then the specific therapeutic skills, and finally, the ways in which therapists can obtain training.

Basic Values and Assumptions

Virginia's inherent respect for the differences between people also applies to the therapists wishing to use her approach. She appreciates the fact that therapists with very different personalities, styles, and techniques can use her approach productively. She encourages her students and colleagues to be willing to try any learning she has to offer, but to take only what fits for them. Thus, the common bond uniting those who use her approach is not a set of tools but a commitment to the basic assumptions and values that underlie her work.

The first commitment is to an appreciation of life in all its manifestations and a belief that, given the proper conditions, every form of life is oriented towards growth. This belief in the growth model applies to the treatment process, as well as the therapist's own personal goals.

A second commitment is to the assumption that clients have in themselves the seeds of their own growth. In this view, the therapist is like a gardener who knows the optimal conditions for growing beautiful plants and provides the nutrients and cultivation necessary for their growth. Another image is the therapist as a midwife who, by following the person's labor contractions, encourages the birth of new possibilities but is not their creator. The therapist helps the life force to become manifest, but the life force exists independently of him.

A commitment to this assumption creates a paradoxical situation which some therapists have difficulty resolving. Therapists who enter the field intending to rescue suffering clients are assuming the client does not have in himself the resources for change. In Virginia's approach, on the other hand, the client needs to be responsible for himself at all times, and the therapist must abandon the role of rescuer.

The third commitment is to an appreciation for the family process and its struggles and possibilities. Appreciation does not necessarily mean love, but rather a nonjudgmental attitude. The therapist views whatever happens from a multicausal perspective that excludes blame.

The therapist's fourth commitment is to be open and willing to use his humanness as a therapeutic tool. To quote Virginia:

"Using oneself as a therapist is an awesome task. To be equal to that task, one needs to continue to develop one's humanness and maturity. We are dealing with people's lives. In my mind, learning to be a therapist is not like learning to be a plumber. Plumbers can usually settle for techniques. Therapists need to do more. You don't have to love a pipe to fix it. Whatever techniques, philosophy or school of family therapy we belong to, whatever we actually do with others has to be funnelled through ourselves as people.

In my teaching, I focus in depth on the personhood of the therapist. We are people dealing with people.

We need to be able to understand and love ourselves, to be able to look, listen, touch and understand those we see. We need to be able to create the conditions by which we can be looked at, listened to, touched and understood."

Such a commitment has many implications in terms of treatment. The therapist must be willing to use himself as a partner in the process of change. Although an expert with special skills in human relations, the therapist is not superior to family members on a human level. He must be willing constantly to risk exposing his feelings and to trust his internal perceptions when he is not clear about what is happening. Trusting his reactions may be very important diagnostically, even though the therapist may not know what his feelings really mean and may run the risk of having the family react negatively to such input.

A delicate balance is necessary between the family's need to see the therapist as an expert and their awareness of his vulnerability. This means that the therapist must establish his expertise in different ways: by his centeredness, his ability to take leadership, and his active intervention when he becomes aware of destructive forces at work. The therapist's willingness to expose himself also provides a model for the family that feelings are not destructive and that being open to them is a necessary step towards growth.

Using one's ability to be vulnerable as a diagnostic tool contracts sharply to applying some pre-existing theoretical framework to the situation. Trying to make the family fit into the framework may dangerously blind the therapist to other realities in the family in front of his eyes. On the other hand, using one's openness, vulnerability, and feelings as diagnostic tools is scary at the beginning. The therapist may feel that years of learning "how to do therapy" have gone down the drain, rendering him naked, like the emperor without his clothes. As he becomes more familiar with the approach, he realizes it has structure and precision, even if at first it is not apparent.

Essentially, the therapist must be willing to live with the ambiguity of a very dynamic system, in a constant state of flux, with many variables apt to erupt at any time. He will not be able to proceed in an orderly fashion with a slowly evolving treatment plan. He must be able to shift gears instantly, sometimes many times in the course of a session. The external instabilities of the process make it imperative for the therapist to be internally congruent, balanced, and strong. Otherwise, he will not feel comfortable with this approach.

One other important human characteristic of the therapist using this approach is humility. First, the humility of accepting that he does not know what is best for the family or for anyone. Second, the humility of accepting the limitations of relying on his internal perceptions. Examples abound in the session described in Part I of how Virginia checks the accuracy of her interpretations. Thus, the therapist must be willing to trust his intuition as a guideline for working, but not to be stuck with his perceptions.

Finally, the therapist using this approach must be committed to a reverence for the life force and be willing to work toward its positive manifestation. Such an attitude on the part of the therapist means that he recognizes the presence of this life force in every person he sees, even those with the most despicable behavior. He treats every human being with high regard, respect, and awe for his potential.

The humanness of the therapist is described by Virginia:

"It further seems clear to me that whenever we start to try to help another human being, we must necessarily conclude with a deep appreciation of the human soul. Twenty years ago I was very careful to avoid references to the soul because that was in the realm of organized religion and had no place in the 'science' of psychotherapy. Now I think, perhaps, that if religion had really worked, psychiatry might never have been born. I now see the human soul manifesting itself differently. For me, the feeling of the soul is reflected in how we value ourselves as human beings, how we treat our bodies and our emotions and animal and plant life around us. Nurturing is a word that occurs very frequently in my thinking. That is not the same as being dependent or indulging oneself, but rather means a freedom to truly love and value oneself. I doubt whether a really nurtured self can ever abuse that self or inflict abuse on others. Furthermore, I believe that the human soul is really a manifestation of a life force or energy which goes on forming and reforming itself. I believe that we are at the threshold of a breakthrough in tuning into a whole new world of the spirit. I find that people who achieve their sense of self-worth and self-value do not need to 'freeload' on other people. They are clear that their survival is much more based on their ability to clearly know that they are their own total decision-makers as far as managing their own reactions and initiations. They believe in their bones that life is an evolving process, always capable of change."

Human Therapeutic Skills

A therapist committed to the assumptions described above is also willing to keep himself open to his own emotional blocks and to learn more about himself. This section reviews essential human therapeutic skills that the therapist needs to cultivate in order to function effectively. In a growth model, most of these qualities and skills are also needed by the family members in therapy or any other person or system seeking growth and change. As a result, the words therapist and person are used somewhat interchangeably in this section.

The first of these skills is congruence. A congruent person is in touch with his feelings, regardless of what they are. He does not judge them, does not criticize himself for having them, just views them as a thermometer of his inner condition at the moment. By acknowledging what is there, the therapist is in a position to use himself freely; he is better able to see, hear, and make decisions without being encumbered by an inner dialogue. In addition to being aware of his feelings, the congruent person takes responsibility for them and does not put the blame outside himself for having them.

If the first step towards congruence is recognizing one's feelings, the second step is recognizing that one has choices about what to do with them. Sometimes it may be wise to express the feelings, at others it may be healthier not to. Timing is very important in that respect: it would indeed be a mistake for a husband who is angry at his wife for forgetting to pay the mortgage to let her know when she is in a hurry to leave for work, or for a

therapist to tell a father at the beginning of a first therapeutic session that she is experiencing feelings of sadness because he reminds her of her husband who had
recently died. Obviously, if those feelings interfere with
the treatment process, they will eventually have to be
dealt with. What is important is that the congruent person is aware of the context in which his feelings exist
and responds to those feelings in a manner that fits the
context. People are often afraid of their feelings because
they are unaware of the freedom they have to choose
how to respond to their feelings. This lack of awareness
is, unfortunately, a result of an educational process that
does not distinguish between an unacceptable behavior
and a feeling. The child who throws a rock at his brother
must be taught that such behavior is unacceptable and
that he needs to develop different methods for coping
with his anger. Instead, he is often taught that it is bad
to have angry feelings.

Congruence is an important prerequisite for keeping
centered. Being centered means that one is able to focus
entirely on the present situation, without concern for
what lies ahead. If a person who is about to deliver a
very important lecture becomes so preoccupied by the
lecture that he fails to notice an oncoming car and has
a head-on collision, his concern about a future event has
prevented him from being centered. The same problem
could occur in therapy, especially during the stage of
chaos. If the therapist becomes concerned about anything other than the immediate, he can not attend to
each of the steps needed to move from the known to
the unknown.

The therapist also needs to know when he loses objec-
tivity and no longer feels balanced and in charge. His

main task then consists of becoming centered again, before making any other attempts at working with the family. Virginia feels so strongly about the need for centeredness that she starts most of her workshops or training sessions by a meditation, or centering exercise, intended to bring everyone's focus into the present, separating them from past and future concerns.

The therapist's ability to check on his own internal manifestations is one of the most important therapeutic tools he has. If his internal experience of the interview is different from all the other data he is observing and he is fairly sure his reaction is not related to something going on in his own life, then the most effective way to proceed is on the basis of that internal data. It takes time for the therapist to become aware and to be able to trust his internal manifestations, but when he does, he will always have another way to proceed in a therapy situation when he feels stuck.

In addition to being able to respond to internal signals, the therapist must also be aware of what his bodily posture may express about his feelings toward the family. For instance, if he becomes aware that he is slumping increasingly in his chair, he needs to check if working with this family is depressing to him.

The effective therapist relies on his sensory channels. His ability to see, hear, feel, smell, and taste needs to be developed, operating, and clear. The more the therapist is able to rely on his senses, the more accurately he will be able to observe what is happening and the less he will need to make deductions about the multiple behavioral and bodily clues to which he is exposed. He needs to be able to observe the congruency between family members' body messages and their words, tone, and quality of expression. He needs to be able to relate their body movements to what else is happening at the moment. Keen senses are an important asset.

As the therapist develops these qualities and skills in himself, he is also able to model them for his clients. The most important modeling is probably the therapist's willingness to risk exposing his feelings without knowing what the feelings really mean or how the family will react. He thus is able to model for the family that feelings are not destructive but can be used for growth because their expression insures an open system.

Training

How can therapists interested in using this approach acquire the necessary skills and qualities? To date, Virginia does not have a formal school or training institute to certify therapists. Most people who consider themselves her students have attended a minimum of one month of intensive training in a residential setting. Some have worked with her over a number of years in a variety of settings. Out of this group, along with other people Virginia considers her peers, she has formed the Avanta Network. Although the majority of the Network is comprised of family therapists, several members represent other disciplines. Virginia describes the common bond for members as a commitment to the "Seven Cs":

Commitment, which means having a philosophy that a human being is the priority, and that our work and our living go toward that end.

Congruence, which essentially means we are going in the direction of being honest, with our insides matching our outsides.

Compatibility, which means that we can have a human relationship with everyone we meet.

Competence, which means we use the information from different kinds of learnings to keep building a fuller and fuller self, with increasing skills and understandings about the human being.

Cooperation, which means that people build with one another instead of dividing and competing.

Compassion, which means feeling with and for another person, to be able to stand in his or her shoes.

Consciousness, which means being aware of our relatedness to the universal life force.

Community, which means that we recognize we are a basic part of the human and environmental context.

The Avanta Network has enabled Virginia to expand her training resources, in that many Avantans are trainers using her general approaches. Some members of the Network even have their own Family Training Institutes for students of family therapy. (It is important to add that a number of Virginia's students are not members of the Avanta Network but are committed to the "Seven Cs" in their treatment of families as well as in their training of family therapists.) Information about these Family Training Institutes can be obtained from the Avanta Network, P.O. Box 7402, Menlo Park, CA 94025.

Since 1980 and in collaboration with the Avanta Network, Virginia has conducted an annual Process Community. This intensive four-week training experience combines personal growth with the study of the specific skills and techniques that constitute the basis of her approach. Participants are exposed to a combination of didactic and experiential learnings. These two types of learning are not separated in Virginia's teachings: when expanding on the more theoretical aspects of her training (some of the concepts described in chapter 1), she anchors her teaching by an experiential component. By the same token, she puts experiential learnings into a theoretical framework that explains the rationale behind their use.

Specifically, the trainees gain experience in the following areas: first, in sensory and body awareness, enabling them to listen to cues in their own body, as well as to become better observers of those cues in others; and second, in developing congruence in communication, thereby being able to become more aware and open about their feelings, while at the same time developing more precision in their communication.

Participants as well as trainers spend considerable training time in triads. As explained earlier, Virginia views working in a triad as an opportunity to resolve the residual problems of one's triad of origin (Ma, Pa, and child), as well as a training ground for understanding family dynamics. Some training takes place in small groups where the participants, under the leadership of an Avanta triad, have an opportunity to practice and work through problems of a personal, familial, or professional nature. Triads can be considered family subgroups, while the small group mirrors problems occurring in a family of more than three. Finally, training in the entire group can represent work at a community level. For most individuals, these three settings parallel the contexts of their own lives.

The focal point of the last two weeks is on the Family Reconstruction technique and, to a lesser extent, the Parts Party (see next chapter). Family reconstruction is a powerful dramatic experience that enables us to make discoveries about our families and our psychological roots. We tend to reproduce in our current lives the learnings of our childhood, but often they no longer fit our present context. By revisiting the sources of these old learnings, we can look at them with new eyes and discard those that create problems for us.

The therapist needs to distinguish clearly between what gets activated in him around an issue of his own past, and what is activated in the family members he works with. In other words, it is important that the therapist be aware of—or, even better, that he work through—unresolved issues that interfere with his ability to remain centered around the issues brought up by the family. This is the reason that the family reconstruction is one of the key turning points of training for the family therapist.

Trainees have an opportunity to learn by watching a family reconstruction. Many have an opportunity to participate in one, and a few have the privilege of having theirs done, either by Virginia or by a leadership triad. Working as part of a triad and having one's family reconstruction done are akin to what a training analysis represents for a traditional psychoanalyst. Therefore, it is imperative that a serious student of Virginia's approach seek an opportunity to have his family reconstruction done (there are a number of qualified "family reconstructionists" in the United States and abroad. Their names can be obtained from the Avanta Network; see page 235.)

The training at the Process Community has been described in such detail because it is an excellent example
of the process Virginia uses in any in-depth workshop.
This approach to training is the definitive antidote to the
cookie-cutter approach.

Chapter 6
Tools and
Techniques

My initial thought when I decided to include this chapter on tools and techniques was that it would be easy to write. I would simply describe some of the techniques or exercises frequently used by Virginia and by Avantans when they do family therapy or conduct workshops on the general theme of making positive changes in a variety of organizations and groups. When I finally started to write this chapter, several months later, I realized that my initial plan violated the spirit of Virginia's whole approach to therapy and change. Such a chapter would give the impression that to use technique X, all one had to do was follow the instructions. I have heard Virginia state over and over again that although specific techniques are useful, what is most important is the way people feel about themselves and about the possibilities for change.

I therefore changed my approach. Rather than writing a step-by-step description of techniques, I have explained the context in which they are used and what they try to accomplish. I think the best introduction to the way in which techniques fit into the Satir approach is a story reported by John D. Stevens in the foreword of *Frogs into Princes:*

"There is an old story of a boilermaker who was hired to fix a huge steamship boiler system that was not working well. After listening to the engineer's description of the problems and asking a few questions, he went to the boiler room. He looked at the maze of twisting pipes, listened to the thump of the boiler and the hiss of escaping steam for a few minutes, and felt some pipes with his hands. Then he hummed softly to himself, reached into his overalls and took out a small hammer, and tapped a bright red valve, once. Immediately, the entire system began working perfectly, and the boilermaker went home. When the steamship owner received a bill for $1,000 he complained that the boilermaker had only been in the engine room for fifteen minutes, and requested an itemized bill. This is what the boilermaker sent to him:

For tapping with hammer: $ .50
For knowing where to tap: 999.50
                                  $1,000.00"

For Virginia, knowing where and how to tap is more important than the tapping itself. In fact, she constantly invents new ways of helping families and family members to see themselves and their connections in a new light. Thus, her ways are unique because they are specially adapted each time to particular needs and situations.

The word technique as it is used in this chapter is a way of engaging in some specific activity to meet the emergent need of a person or a group of persons *at that moment*. The advantage of using techniques and exercises is that experiential activities maximize the participants' learning and ability to use that learning for change. Living through an experience engages one's total person rather than just one part, such as one's brains or emotions. Techniques involve new ways of looking at one's own and others' behavior: the implicit can be made explicit, the unfamiliar can be made familiar, the verbally inexpressible can be expressed, and new awarenesses can be developed.

To be meaningful, techniques need to be tailor-made for the situation. Otherwise, they should not be used at all. The chief danger lies in using techniques as cookie cutters regardless of the amount, consistency, or texture of the dough, or using them as time-fillers with the hope that they will be of benefit. Using techniques in such a fashion brings to mind the statement attributed to Abraham Maslow: "If your only tool is a hammer, it is difficult not to see every problem as a nail." Even when the problem *is* a nail, it is crucial to know precisely when, how, and where to tap.

Techniques need to be used with flexibility. At times, a need emerges in the middle of using a specific technique, or a different course of action may suddenly seem more appropriate. It is also important that the therapist be very flexible as to the outcome, which is very often unpredictable. So, although the therapist has a goal in mind when he starts, he needs to be ready for whatever the outcome of the intervention may be.

Most tools used by Virginia developed from something accidental or some need of the moment. The first time she used a simulated family was in 1962 at a welfare conference in Colorado, when the family she was about to interview failed to show up.

"I found this out and when I got over the panic that ensued, I said to myself, 'All right, Virginia, if you are so smart about family systems, you ought to be able to make a simulated family.' Somewhere from the back of my head came the design. I tried it and it not only worked, it became the model that I have used ever since. I use this when I work with groups of families. I put students who are learning family therapy in different kinds of simulated families and I also use this model when I do family reconstruction."

Having issued these warnings, I would like to take a more positive approach. The remainder of this chapter will cover, first, some of the questions that go through the therapist's mind before making a decision on the use of a specific approach or intervention. Second, after some generalizations about major elements in the techniques used in Virginia's approach, several techniques are described. Third, it discusses similarities and differences in the use of such tools during family therapy and workshops.

Deciding How to Proceed

There are as many different ways to decide how to proceed with a therapeutic situation as there are therapists. Usually a number of choices exist. The therapist's thinking process may vary, but he needs to ask himself certain key questions:

What is going on right now, with this person, family, or group?

What is present but not manifest?

What needs to be changed?

What would I like to accomplish?

What would be a good way to accomplish the immediate goal I see right at this moment?

What resources do I have at my disposal in terms of time, people, and context?

Are individual family members ready for the experience that is developing in my mind?

Will this experience achieve the expected outcome, or would another one fit better?

Needless to say, this is a "thinking on one's feet" process. The above questions are not so explicitly drawn out, especially by an experienced therapist. When a therapist does not have the answers to these questions, progress will be difficult. It would be easy to run into some of the problems described earlier in this chapter.

Major Elements in Virginia's Techniques

Most of Virginia's techniques originated in her fertile mind or were stimulated by interaction with many New Consciousness thinkers and practitioners. When exposed to a new idea that fits, she finds some way to incorporate it in a manner meaningful to others. Virginia's uncanny ability to translate arcane theoretical concepts makes the theory come alive.

Before describing the specific tools and techniques used by Virginia, it seems appropriate to comment on several elements that appear in many of her interventions. They are the use of sculpture, metaphor, drama, reframing, humor, and touch.

Sculpture*

For family members, experiential activities bring the family system to life by making explicit the patterns that

*Virginia developed the sculpturing and posturing techniques in 1965. They have been greatly expanded since that time.

family members know implicitly. Sculpture is one of the most representative experiential activities used by Virginia. Based on her image of what is going on in the family, she asks family members to sculpt their relationships to each other, using gestures and bodily pictures together with components of distance and closeness, which show the communication and relationship patterns. Sometimes each family member is asked to sculpt his own picture, which gives other members a chance to realize that they may have different pictures of their family system. When movement is introduced, the sculpture becomes a ballet.

One advantage of a sculpture is that, as a behavioral demonstration, it is much more accurate in what it reflects about family communications than a verbal description. Another advantage is that it makes past experiences alive in the present. It is important to stress that although Virginia is a very directive leader in this process, she always carefully checks with the protagonists to make sure that her interpretation fits their inner reality.

Metaphor

Webster's defines a metaphor as "a figure of speech in which a word or phrase literally denoting one kind of object or idea is used in place of another to suggest a likeness or analogy between them." A metaphor is being used, then, each time an image or association is transposed from one arena to another in order to highlight similarities, differences, or ambiguities. The use of metaphors can develop new awarenesses by connecting or linking two events, ideas, characteristics, or meanings, and transforming experiences from one mode to another. Metaphors are not limited to figures of speech, but can be found in many areas of living. For example, when a therapist observes a child playing with a doll ("How often have I told you not to eat with your fingers?") and uses that observation to make inferences about how this child feels treated by his mother, a metaphor is involved.

Virginia often uses the metaphor of a pot when she is referring to feelings of self-worth, because of the way in which people refer to such feelings in quantitative terms. She came to this because of the way her family used their big iron pot on their farm in Wisconsin. The pot was used for making soap part of the year. When threshing crews came in the summer, the pot was filled with stew. At other times it was used to store manure and was called the "3-S pot." Whenever anyone wanted to use the pot, he was faced with two questions: What is the pot now full of, and how full is it?

When Virginia compares the way so many families conduct themselves to a can of worms, she is using a metaphor for the seemingly purposeless contortions families often get involved in. Communication stances in which people adopt various postures, provide a metaphor for expressing inside feelings through outside manifestations.

There are many positive aspects to the use of metaphors. They enable one to give information in a non-threatening manner by allowing a certain distancing from the situation. They allow the creation of imagery which reinforces learning.

Drama

Family members or workshop participants are asked to play out a scene from their own or somebody else's life. The language of drama—the use of pantomime, spacial relationships, and sculpture—allows for the expression of internal images which go far beyond the linear description of a situation when it is stated in words. It also allows for the metaphorical expression of inner states otherwise difficult to express. Participants have an opportunity to return to a situation or to know about the life of another person from the inside. This allows them to look at the situation with new eyes and enables them to achieve new insights and develop new connections with the people they relate to.

Reframing

Virginia often reframes problematic behaviors and responses and makes explicit the positive intentions and positive by-products underlying them. The purpose of the reframe is to create a shift in the perceptions of family members with respect to the behavior so that it may be handled more constructively. Comments 25 and 26 are examples of reframing. For elaboration on this approach, see these books by Richard Bandler and John Grinder: *Frogs into Princes, Reframing,* and (in collaboration with Virginia Satir) *Changing with Families.*

Humor

Humor is another important ingredient in Virginia's approach to therapy. She often uses it in making contact with family members (comment 3), which contributes to the creation of a relaxed and friendly atmosphere. During sculpting or developing a ballet of family interactions, humor is usually present many times. Virginia will not hesitate even during the most intense interaction to add a light touch if the situation warrants it. The stress ballet of Margie and Casey is an example of a powerful therapeutic and learning experience facilitated by the humorous context of the situation, which enables them both to be aware of their behavior without needing to be defensive about it. Laughter is a powerful therapeutic tool which can transform the way in which a family looks at itself.

Touch

During the course of her work with a family, Virginia often touches family members. She is aware of the powerful impact of physical contact, and she usually starts an interview by reaching for every family member's hand. It is important to stress, however, that her touch is not an automatic, mechanistic "technique" that she uses indiscriminately. She is very sensitive to cues she receives about people's boundaries and will not transgress them. Her touch is always a response to an invitation, at least at a subliminal level. After she has established a rapport with individual family members, she uses physical touch more freely, often as a source of nonverbal support when she is engaged verbally with another family member (comments 49 and 84). To quote Virginia:

"My hands are my most valuable treatment asset. Also my body and my skin, in sensing what is going on; and my eyes in seeing; and the connections that all of these make. Hands are *so* important! This is one of the reasons I try to help people to educate their hands. Something else I do in affectional relationships with people is to help them to educate their bodies and also to be aware of space and boundaries. I am quite convinced that that's what this business of making connections really means. What I have just said helps me make a definition of intimacy. It is simply the freedom to respect the spaces between people—to go in when there is an invitation, and not to invade when there isn't one. That is real intimacy."

Tools and Techniques

Below are descriptions of several techniques often used by Virginia and Avantans when they do family therapy and conduct workshops. These techniques are sometimes used in the way I describe here; sometimes they are modified, shortened, or integrated with other techniques. The only limits to the ways they can be used are in the imagination of the user.

Rather than giving very specific details on how to do these techniques, I focus on the goals they try to accomplish. The means to those ends are merely examples. The imagination of the therapist and the emergent possibilities of the situation can add new creativity and create new techniques.

Family reconstruction is elaborated more than other techniques because it embodies the quest for meaning which is at the core of Virginia's work.

Communication Stances*

The communication stances are a basic technique used in family therapy or in workshops, either in their pure form or integrated into another technique (simulated family, family reconstruction, etc.). These stances bring to life five of the basic interactional patterns found in families all over the world: placating, blaming, computing, being irrelevant, and being congruent. In groups of three to five, family members or workshop partici-

*These were developed in 1964 by Virginia Satir.

pants position themselves in postures representing these communication modes. They caricaturize the physical postures that accompany the verbal expressions of these interactional patterns. For example, a placating person would be asked to kneel in an awkward, off-balance position, head looking up, shoulders bowed as if begging someone to rescue him and be his reason for living. A blaming person would be asked to stand in an accusatory stance with an extended finger. A computing person would stand straight, as if he had a rod in his back, while the irrelevant person would appear completely disconnected—his body constantly spinning, each limb moving in a different direction—and unaware of what he was doing.

By adopting these positions in sequence, participants become aware of their preferred interactional pattern, its meaning for themselves, and its meaning in relation to others. They discover the meaning of the incongruence that occurs when a person's internal feelings do not match his external expression of them.

These stances are also an excellent way to demonstrate to a family or workshop participants how the family system is based on these communication patterns. For further discussion see chapters 5 and 6 of *Peoplemaking* and Part Four of *Conjoint Family Therapy*.

Family Stress Ballet

The family stress ballet is an extension of the communication stances. Participants are asked to shift positions in rapid succession, as they might in a real-life situation. This shifting can be done either under the direction of the therapist or spontaneously, according to the participants' sense of what is going on. An excellent demonstration of the stress ballet is given by Casey and

Margie, who discover a pattern to their seemingly un-related communications (comments 117–120). The goal of the stress ballet is to demonstrate to the participants the high cost of incongruent communications to the family system and to the individuals with it.

Simulated Family

A simulated family is created by asking unrelated participants in a workshop to form families and to assume the roles of family members. Someone who has not participated in one of these simulated families might easily dismiss it as inconsequential role playing, since it does not deal with reality. The simulated family is a very powerful technique, however, because it is based on the universality of the communication stances, which rapidly produce in a simulated family the stresses that exist in a real family that uses these communication patterns. The experience of being in a simulated family helps one to understand the power and universality of the family system.

Family simulations are used in a variety of settings to teach about a number of characteristics of family systems. A very facilitative training and teaching instrument, they are often used in workshops or demonstrations. They are sometimes used in a "fishbowl" format, giving the audience a chance to share their reactions to what they observe. Family simulations are also invaluable in teaching real families about themselves. This can be done by asking family members to simulate each other's behaviors, so that the mother can show the father how she sees him acting and vice versa; or, by having a chance to step into his shoes, she may get a better understanding of his behavior. There are, of course, multiple variations on this theme.

Ropes as a Therapeutic Tool

Used as a metaphor for relationships, ropes can serve to make the family network come alive for its members. This technique is an excellent way to demonstrate how one part of the family system affects the rest of the system. Each family member receives a short rope, the "self" rope, to attach around his or her waist. In addition, each receives as many ropes as there are other family members. He ties these ropes, which represent his relationships to every other family member, around his own waistline rope. Then, each family member hands the appropriate relationship rope to the family member to whom it belongs. Each family member is thus encumbered by all the ropes representing his relationship to other family members as well as by all the ropes representing their relationships to him.

The purpose of this technique is to demonstrate to the participants, as well as observers, the importance of using these ropes judiciously. Otherwise, they can create tremendous entanglements and tensions. Family members often do not realize that there is no way in which they can be attentive to every family member at the same time, and that they need the freedom to move in their family relations. These ropes can bring out the same feelings in participants as those they experience in their daily life when they are not attached by ropes. By becoming aware of what happens when they learn how to relax the tension of the ropes, they can transfer this learning to the real situation.

Ropes can also be used as a metaphor for illustrating other types of interaction, connections, or relationships when one wants to raise participants' awareness or demonstrate how to transform tension and stress into a more relaxed state.

Anatomy of a Relationship

The anatomy of a relationship is a technique that helps couples become aware of the way in which their unspoken, usually unconscious, marriage contract affects their family life and their relationship as a couple. This unspoken contract usually consists of a combination of dreams and fantasies about the ideal relationship, combined with the deep-seated needs that each partner brings to the marriage. For instance, one of the fantasies that a misunderstanding of the Bible has fostered is that the ideal of marriage is to "be as one." This unrealistic expectation makes it impossible to negotiate the very difficult balance of the "me, you, and us" that is part of every healthy relationship.

Some basic stances can be sculpted to demonstrate the marital contract's possible variations and its outcomes for the couple and their children. This is done by asking a man and a woman (they can be a real couple, or volunteers from an audience, depending on the context) to sculpt the interaction. An example of such a contract might be between a couple for whom one of the initial attractions was that the husband was a strong individual who liked to take care of people, while his wife liked the idea that she had found somebody that she could lean on. This would be represented by the man standing straight and looking ahead, with the woman standing behind him, leaning on his back, her arms extended around his neck. If she spoke, her words would be, "You are my big hero," which would boost his ego. The woman is then asked to increase her pull, thus increasing pressure on the man's back to the point where he develops a "pain in the neck" or his back begins to hurt, especially when he tries to move and feels that "she is a drag" on his shoulders. As children come into the situation, the weight on the shoulders of the husband/father usually increases, creating pressures that can result in a variety of consequences. The same situation could be reversed, with the husband leaning on his wife. This is just one example of the implicit contract that could exist for a couple.

The anatomy of a relationship can be very effective as a diagnostic tool. Each partner in the couple can be asked first to sculpt the way he sees himself in relation to the other, and then to sculpt the way he would like the relationship to be.

Family Reconstruction*

Of all the techniques developed by Virginia, family reconstruction is probably the most representative of her theories on how people evolve and change. Like so many other techniques, it shares elements of other schools (general systems theory, communications theory, group dynamics, group process, psychodrama, gestalt therapy, and psychoanalytic theory, to name a few). The end result, however, is a very powerful therapeutic and learning experience with a character all its own.

Three goals are essential to a family reconstruction. The first is to reveal to a person the source of his old learnings. Since the people who assumed responsibility for our development often had very different ideas, we received mixed messages about what was going on or what was expected from us when we were growing up. In trying to make sense of these contradictions, we often developed a distorted view of reality because many pieces were missing to the puzzle of living. In addition, the adults around us were usually very concerned about

*Family Reconstruction was fully developed by Virginia by 1968. The beginnings were in 1964.

how we developed physically, intellectually, and mor-
ally, but often neglected the development of our emotional tools. For instance, when a child notices an expression of sorrow or sadness on a parent's face, asks
what is going on, and hears: "Nothing, just go out and
play," he is left with a big question mark. In attempting
to find an answer, the child will probably come up with
a very distorted idea about what motivated his parent
and how to explain that behavior. As a result, this child,
like most children, will grow up with a lot of nonsense
that he accepted as fact. This is not the result of any
malevolence on the part of parents, but is due to the fact
that most parents seem to be ignorant of, or behave as
if they were unaware of, the fact that their children, even
when small, are human beings able to hear, smell,
touch, feel, and think. Three principles seem to govern
the actions of most parents: (1) Adults should not burden children and should shield them from ugliness and
evil; (2) Adults should set examples of their ideas of
perception, which often include rules such as, "I should
always be cheerful and strong"; and (3) Children are too
young to understand.

Through the process of family reconstruction, the person—called the Star for the duration of this process—
has an opportunity to reconstruct the past mysteries of
his life and find missing pieces of the puzzle. He has an
opportunity to return to his parent's sadness, to reawaken his past reaction to it, and to come away with a
new understanding of what actually happened, distinct
from what he perceived or misconstrued at the time.

The second goal is for the Star to develop an awareness of the personhood of his parents. Many people
carry throughout life the picture they had formed of
their parents when they depended on them for their

survival. This gives them a distorted view of what their parents are or were like as human beings—all the way from the one extreme of making them heroes bigger than life to the other, in which they are miserable weaklings. Sometimes one parent may be viewed as a saint, while the other appears to be a devil (Margie provides a good example of this contrast in comment 57).

The third goal is for the Star to pave the way for finding his own personhood. As the Star begins to understand the missing pieces that distorted his view of reality and is able to look at his parents with the eyes of an adult, he can begin to develop a new model for living by transforming the old model into something more in keeping with existence as a whole human being. If great gaps exist between him and his parents, as often happens, he may also learn to develop new ways to enjoy a more nurturing relationship with them.

A family reconstruction needs to take place in a group setting, usually with enough members to provide a separate actor for each family member (about ten to twenty participants). Whenever possible, sex roles should be respected.

An essential step in preparing for a family reconstruction is to make a chronological account of the family's history, from the birth of the oldest grandparent to the present day, noting only events. The Guide, who leads the Star through the reconstruction, asks questions based on the calendar rather than on the Star's memory. This forces the Star to focus on events he might have otherwise forgotten, taking into account the fact that our minds often sift out significant events and fuse them, thus giving us an inaccurate picture of cause and effect.

This chronology yields an orderly account of what has happened in the family. In addition to family events such as births, deaths, moves, marriages, etc., it includes other events which hold personal significance for the Star, even though they may not seem important to others. In noting these events, the Star indicates the specific time, place, and setting, including who was present and what they were doing. He also indicates world events which served as context for the specific family happenings.

Another important part of the preparation is for the Star to develop a Family Map. The Family Map is a spatial or graphic indication of the family organization for three generations, proceeding from the birth of the Star's oldest grandparent. The Star fills in all names and notes five to six adjectives for each character according to his perception of them or the perceptions he has learned from his family. If the Star does not remember the name, he can make it up. The preparation of the map already provides some learning experiences for the Star in terms of seeing the organization of the characters who make up his past.

A third element that can be used is the Circle of Influence. Putting himself in the middle of a circle, the Star draws spokes towards all the people who played a significant role and influenced his development in his growing-up years. The thickness of the spoke is related to the importance that the Star attributes to the relationship.

It is essential that a trusting relationship exist between the Star and the Guide before starting the reconstruction. The Guide needs to spend time with the Star before the actual reconstruction starts in order to become entirely familiar with the information brought out during the preparation. Based on this information, the Guide selects certain scenes to maximize the Star's learning from this process. This is where the art of the Guide comes in.

The reconstruction itself is a form of drama. Its essential scenes are:

1. The family life history of each of the people who became the Star's parents. This concerns the people who became the Star's grandparents.
2. The meeting, courtship, and marriage story of the people who became the Star's parents.
3. The advent of the children of this union, with emphasis on the Star's birth.

Enacting the childhood of each of the Star's parents illuminates the old learnings that they received, which opens the way to understanding their personhood and their spouse selection as well as subsequent interactions. Portraying their meeting, courtship, and marriage illuminates the Star's opportunity to see his parents as human and understandable people with whom he can easily identify. It also makes it possible for the Star to understand the covert contract that led to the later pain with which the Star is usually more familiar. Developing the Star's own family now enables the Star to look at new learnings with new eyes.

The Guide uses every opportunity for which he has information to illuminate past events, to connect them with the Star's feelings of self-esteem, and to pave the way for new learnings. As the Star comes to the awareness that he is using outmoded ways of coping with his life, he becomes free to leave them and to behave in ways that fit for him now, to act from choice rather than compulsion.

Sometimes it is not possible to do the Family Reconstruction as described above. With children who were
adopted or grew up in orphanages, for instance, the
Guide deals with the information available in order to
help the Star look at the story he had made up for
himself with new eyes.*

Parts Party

The goals of a Parts Party are to help a person become aware that he is made up of many different parts,
get acquainted with them, understand them, and learn
how to use them in an harmonious and integrated manner. We all have a number of different parts, each with
expectations of fulfillment. These parts often find it difficult to get along with each other and may have inhibi-
tory influences on one another. We like some parts,
which have proven useful to us and which we may wish
to expand. There are some parts we do not like and we
may find out that when transformed they can be useful
to us. Finally, there are some parts which we may not
be aware of and which can be awakened. The process
of the parts party offers a person an opportunity to
observe these parts and to learn how they can function
more harmoniously when they cooperate rather than
compete.

An individual's parts develop from the experiences he
has from birth as well as through the interpretation that
his mind gives to these experiences. As a result of these
interpretations, each part usually has a positive or negative value attached to it by the owner. To give an exam-

---

*For a more comprehensive presentation of Family Reconstruction see *Your Third
Birth*, to be published in late 1985.

ple, anger often carries a negative connotation or valence because of the early messages an individual received about the expression of such feelings, while aggressiveness can be viewed in positive or negative light depending again on the individual's experiences and interpretations of those experiences. Aggressiveness may be desirable when one needs to devote every effort to achieve a defined goal—for example, in a sport. On the other hand, it could be viewed as a negative characteristic in achieving consensus in a community decision.

In addition, every part carries an aspect of energy which serves to transform it when it understands that it has choices in how and when to manifest itself and that it can cooperate with other parts rather than fighting with them.

A parts party requires a group of at least ten people. The facilitator, called the Guide, asks the Host of the party—the person for whom the party is given—to come up with at least six and no more than ten names of persons, both men and women, preferably in public life, who either attract or repel him but are also interesting enough to invite to a party. The Guide then lists those names on the blackboard and asks the Host to give a simple adjective to each guest personality, thus describing how he feels about each. The Host then selects members of the group to play each part. It is important that each guest understands the Host's unique meaning of each adjective so that he is able to play his part in the way the Host sees it. For instance, if the Host invites John Wayne because of his strength, that character should be played as a strong man rather than any other characteristic that the role-player might see in him.

When all the guests understand their roles, the Guide asks them to come to the party, dramatizing their respective personalities and adjectives in an exaggerated way. The experience is divided in the following sequences: meeting the parts, witnessing their conflict, transforming them, and integrating them.

1. Meeting the parts. First, the Host meets his guests and observes how they interact with each other. As soon as the guests form the first clusters, the Guide freezes the action and simply points out to the Host which personality is with whom: "John Wayne, your strength, may be standing next to Cleopatra, your sexiness," etc. After this, the Guide directs the party to continue, freezing the parts where new clusters are formed and pointing out each time simply what is happening.

2. Witnessing the conflict between the parts. When there are obvious signs of struggle in one or several clusters, the Guide freezes the action and asks only one of the clusters to talk. The Host listens closely and then comments on the familiarity of the conflict. If the Host is familiar with the dialogue, the Guide asks for increased action. If the Host does not claim familiarity, the party goes on until another struggle is located with which the Host feels familiar. Each part (at some point during the party, the role players loose their names and just become the characteristics they represent) is then asked to state what is going on as well as how he feels about what is going on, while the Host is asked to listen carefully.

The Guide then directs all the parts to try to dominate the party by asking them to take obvious action and not just talk. Again the Host is asked to comment about the familiarity of what is happening. When the action becomes clear, the Guide freezes the action and asks each part to tell what his plans are and what each needs to make his plan work.

When each part tries to dominate the party, it is impossible for any plan to work, because divisions and chaos prevent any constructive action. The next step then is to turn to the parts and ask them what they need in order to be more comfortable in the situation.

3. Transforming the parts. The parts are now becoming aware that they need cooperation from some other part in order to have their needs met. For instance, sexuality might say that if ambition and intelligence were not holding him down so tightly, he might have a chance to bring some joy to his hosting part. Ambition might reply that if he listened to sexuality, he would never achieve anything. Intelligence might add that sexuality might do dumb things if left on his own. Again, the Host is asked to comment about his feelings regarding the situation.

These three parts will then be asked to find a way of helping each other so that they can maximize their value to their owner. They usually find that by cooperating rather than warring, they not only succeed at their objective but also become much more comfortable. Often cooperation can be attained only by a transformation of destructive into constructive energy. As an example, ambition sometimes leads people into some "man eat man" types of actions. When tempered by intelligence and care, however, the negative energy that leads to a destructive mode can become transformed into the positive energy that allows a person to move ahead and be an effective leader. The same is true with any other part that carries a negative valence for its owner.

A similar process takes place with all parts until they all feel comfortable. Occasionally it becomes clear that no resolution can be achieved for one or several of the parts without adding another part (or more). For instance, the owner of the parts may suddenly realize that he forgot to invite wisdom. If this happens, someone from the audience may be asked to step in and be wisdom, thus enabling the resolution of remaining conflicts. Usually, the part was not missing beforehand but was lying dormant. Through the process of the parts party, the Host has an opportunity to realize that in his life he must always make sure that wisdom is present when he needs it.

4. Integrating the parts. After all the parts feel that they have acquired a place in the sun and that they can function harmoniously with one another, they are asked to form a circle around their owner. The Host is then asked to get in touch with his feelings and verbalize them. One by one from their places in the circle, the parts move in front of the Host and introduce themselves in their transformed states ("I am your ability to make decisions," for example). After all have spoken, the Host is then asked to accept his parts formally, one by one. He then closes his eyes and again gets in touch with and verbalizes his feelings. Each part is directed to announce himself, simultaneously touching the Host with his hands until all parts are connected by hand to their owner. Once more the Host is asked to connect with and verbalize his feelings. Quietly, the Guide directs each part to take his hands off the Host. Eyes still closed, the Host is asked one last time to assess his feelings and verbalize them.

Many different parts can be used in a parts party, depending on where the focus seems to be needed. It is possible to invite different parts of the body, for example, when the Host has cut off feelings there. A parts party can also be done with different aspects of a human being, such as mind, feelings, body, interactions, and soul. The basic idea remains the same: to help people become aware of their resources and find ways to use them more effectively, either in their present state or by transforming them. The Host can also become aware that he has choices as to when and how to use his parts and that their energy can be transformed so that they become assets rather than liabilities.

Parts parties can be adapted to many situations. When the Star in a family reconstruction has difficulty dealing with and integrating three different aspects of his father, it may be useful to ask three role-players to represent those parts and interact with each other. In individual therapy, a client could be the sole actor for all the parts in his party.*

Exercises for Awareness Enhancement

Over the years, Virginia has developed a number of exercises aimed at developing the participants' awareness in several areas. Briefly discussed here are two general areas of exercises which are often used by Virginia and are an essential part of her approach to changing awareness.

The first is the area of the "affective domain," which helps participants become aware of how often they do

*For a greater discussion in depth see *Your Third Birth*, to be published in late 1985.

not make effective use of their senses and helps them develop sensory awareness. Usually conducted in dyads and generally used as a series of interactions, these exercises show people concretely and experientially what happens when they do or do not look, touch, and speak, and how this affects their communication.

The second general area is that of triadic exercises. Over the years, Virginia has developed a number of exercises intended to make participants discover or rediscover the power of the triad. In some instances, these exercises consist of using communication stances in triadic situations to make participants aware of what happens to them. Other exercises help a person realize how he feels when he is included or excluded from an interaction involving two other people and how these feelings can be different, depending on the way in which he is ignored. In another kind of exercise, one participant is asked to play the role of an infant or child and to report how he feels when confronted by mixed messages from his parents in a variety of situations. In addition to making people aware of all the potential difficulties of triadic interactions, it is also essential to give them experiences that demonstrate the tremendous possibilities and resources offered by the triad.

Using Techniques in Context

So far in this chapter, we have referred to tools and techniques used in family therapy. It is important to state that all the techniques described in this chapter can be used in whole or in part in a variety of contexts and settings as long as the therapist is aware of the difference in focus. At the basis of family therapy is a therapeutic contract: an agreed upon understanding between all the involved parties as to what will be explored and the rights and responsibilities of all persons. Too often, however, the therapist assumes this contract exists merely by virtue of the usual helper-helpee relationship. If people come to the therapist, then they must be ready and willing to be helped. Nothing could be farther from the truth. People—in the case of families, family members—are probably not only somewhat ambivalent about the process, but have different expectations and understandings about it. They also are at different stages of readiness and have different fears and anxieties about it. These feelings need to be recognized and acknowledged, and some agreement must be reached about how much each is willing to participate and how far each is willing to go. Failure to deal with this phase usually creates problems down the road. Virginia pays special attention to the contract phase and uses it both diagnostically and therapeutically.

In a workshop, the therapeutic contract is replaced by a learning contract. This means that most participants are present because they want to learn something. That some participants are present because they want therapy, and that therapy actually takes place in many instances, does not alter the fact that there is a different emphasis in terms of the desired outcomes. For example, the communication stances that Virginia has developed are often used to bring a family's awareness to the relationship patterns in their interactions that interfere with smooth family functioning. The purpose of using the communication stances is to bring about new perceptions and an awareness about the possibility of change. When communication stances are used in a workshop, the purpose is to make participants aware of their own use of the various styles, while illustrating communication patterns that can take place in a family. Of course, behavioral changes may take place as a result of the change in awareness.

It could be pointed out quite appropriately that Family Reconstruction would not be used in family therapy. This is true if we think of Family Reconstruction as a monolithic piece of work that can only be rigidly applied in one setting. If one focuses on the concepts underlying Family Reconstruction, however, it becomes quite clear that those concepts are often very applicable in working with a family. A good illustration of this point occurs when Virginia asks Casey and Margie to describe their own growing up, to better understand how this affected their parenting. Although no experiential component was involved in that situation, Virginia could well have put them in a role-playing situation to reconstruct their parents. Furthermore, the tools used in preparation for the Family Reconstruction, such as the Family Life Chronology, the Family Map, and the Circle of Influence, are often useful in family therapy.

The converse of this situation is equally true. If, in the middle of some demonstration during a workshop, an individual became disturbed as a result of participating in an experiential situation, Virginia would interrupt the demonstration to deal with the problem on hand.

In conclusion, in this chapter I have described a number of different techniques which are often used by Virginia and her fellow Avantans when they work with families and groups. I have focused on the rationale behind them rather than giving precise information on how they are done. These techniques are meant to grow creatively through the efforts of those who use them. This approach to techniques makes them open-minded and flexible tools, enabling newcomers to add their own creative touches.

Conclusion

My hope for you, the reader, is that the so-called "magic of therapeutic change" so often attributed to me, has been illuminated through the scholarly and comprehensive description contributed by Michele Baldwin.

I am aware that as long as anything remains in the area of magic, it cannot be fruitfully used. Since many people feel drawn to what I do, this book may provide avenues for how to go further on this path

—*Virginia M. Satir*

Bibliography

In addition to references specifically included in this book, this bibliography contains books that have influenced our thinking. You may find them useful in expanding and/or deepening your awareness and knowledge of areas that have merely been touched on in this book.

Ackerman, Nathan. *Psychodynamics of Family Life.* New York: Basic Books, 1958.

Bandler, Richard and John Grinder. *Frogs into Princes.* Moab, UT: Real People Press, 1979.

————. *Reframing.* Moab, UT: Real People Press, 1982.

————. *The Structure of Magic,* vols. I and II. Palo Alto: Science and Behavior Books, 1975.

————, and Virginia Satir. *Changing with Families.* Palo Alto: Science and Behavior Books, 1976.

Bernhard, Yetta. *How to Be Somebody.* Millbrae, CA: Celestial Arts, 1975.

————. *Self-Care.* Millbrae, CA: Celestial Arts, 1975.

Block, Ken. $C = ab - a^2 + a$: *On Becoming a Family.* Unpublished paper, 1978.

Bowen, Murray. *Family Therapy in Clinical Practice.* New York: Jason Aronson, 1978.

————. "Toward the Differentiation of Self in One's Own Family." In J. Framo, ed., *Family Interaction: A Dialogue between Researchers and Family Therapists.* Springer, NY: Springer Pub., 1972.

Brazelton, T. B. *On Becoming a Family: The Growth of Attachment.* New York: Delacorte, 1981.

Buber, Martin. *I and Thou.* New York: Charles Scribner's Sons, 1970.

Burnett-Dixon, Family Reconstruction unpublished dissertation Union Graduate School, Cincinnati, Ohio, 1976.

Buzan, Tony. *Use Both Sides of Your Brain.* New York: E. P. Dutton, 1974.

Caplow, Theodore. *Two Against One: Coalitions in Triads.* Englewood Cliffs, NJ: Prentice Hall, 1969.

Capra, Fritjof. *The Tao of Physics.* New York: Bantam Books, 1977.

Corales, Ramon and Charles B. Bernard. *Theory and Techniques of Family Therapy.* Springfield, IL: Charles C. Thomas, 1979.

Cousins, Norman. *The Anatomy of an Illness.* New York: W. W. Norton, 1979.

————. *The Celebration of Life: Dialogue on Immortality and Infinity.* New York: Harper & Row, 1974.

Dodson, Laura Sue. *Family Counseling: A Systems Approach.* DeWayne Kurpius, ed. Muncie, IN: Accelerated Development, 1977.

Duhl, Bunny S. *From the Inside Out and Other Metaphors.* New York: Brunner-Mazel, 1983.

Duhl, F. J.; D. Kantor; and B. S. Duhl. "Learning, Space and Action in Family Therapy: A Primer of Sculpture." In D. Bloch, ed., *Techniques of Family Psychotherapy.* New York: Grune and Stratton, 1973.

Ford, Frederick R., M.D.; and Joan Herrick, M.S.S. "Family Rules: Family Life Styles." *American Journal of Orthopsychiatry,* January 1974.

Framo, J. L. "Rationale and Techniques of Intensive Family Therapy." In I. Boszormenyi-Nagy and J. L. Framo, eds., *Intensive Family Therapy.* New York: Harper and Row, 1965.

Haley, Jay. *Uncommon Therapy: The Psychiatric Techniques of Milton H. Erickson, M.D.* New York: Norton, 1977.

Horne, Arthur, M. *Family Counseling and Therapy.* Itasca, IL: F. E. Peacock Publishers, 1982.

Jackson, Don D., M.D.; Jules Ruskin, M.D. and Virginia Satir, M.S.W. "A Method of Analysis of a Family Interview." *Archives of General Psychiatry,* Vol. 5, October 1961; pp. 321–40.

Kantor, David and Lehr William. *Inside the Family.* San Francisco: Jossey-Bass, 1975.

LeBoyer, Frederick. *Inner Beauty, Inner Light.* New York: Knopf, 1978.

Lederer, William J. and Don D. Jackson. *Mirages of Marriage.* New York: Norton, 1968.

Luthman, Shirley G. and Martin Kirschenbaum, *The Dynamic Family.* Palo Alto: Science and Behavior Books, 1974.

Maslow, A. H. *Toward a Psychology of Being,* second edition. Princeton, NJ: Van Nostrand, 1968.

Merton, Thomas. *Raids on the Unspeakable.* New York: New Directions, 1964.

MacGregor, Robert; Agnes M. Ritchie; Alberto C. Serrano; and Franklin P. Schuster, Jr. *Multiple-Impact Therapy with Families.* New York: McGraw Hill, 1964.

Minuchin, Salvador. *Families and Family Therapy.* Cambridge, MA: Harvard University Press, 1974.

———— et al. *Families of the Slums: An Exploration of Their Structure Treatment.* New York: Basic Books, 1967.

Montague, Ashley. *Touching: The Human Significance of the Skin.* New York: Columbia University Press, 1971.

Montaigne de, Michel. *Essays.* London: Sampson Low, Marston, Searle, and Rivington, 1880.

Ostrander, Sheila; Lynn Schroeder; with Nancy Ostrander. *Superlearning.* New York: Delacorte/Confucian, 1979.

Papp, P.; O. Silverstein; and E. Carter. "Family Sculpting in Preventive Work with 'Well Families'." In *Family Process,* 12:2 (1973) 197–212.

Pelletier, Kenneth R. *Holistic Medicine.* New York: Delacorte, 1980.

————. *Mind as Healer, Mind as Slayer: A Holistic Approach To Preventing Stress Disorders.* New York: Delacorte/Delta, 1977.

Perls, Frederick S. *Gestalt Therapy Verbatim.* Moab, UT: Real People Press, 1969.

Perls, Fritz. *The Gestalt Approach and Eye Witness to Therapy.* New York: Bantam Books, 1976.

Satir, Virginia. *Conjoint Family Therapy,* third edition. Palo Alto: Science and Behavior Books, 1983.

————. *Peoplemaking.* Palo Alto: Science and Behavior Books, 1972.

————. *Self-Esteem.* Millbrae, CA: Celestial Arts, 1975.

————. *Your Many Faces.* Millbrae, CA: Celestial Arts, 1978.

Satir, Virginia; J. Stachowiak; and H. Taschman. *Helping Families to Change.* New York: Aronson, 1977.

Selye, Hans. *Stress Without Distress.* Philadelphia: J. B. Lippincott, 1974.

————. *The Stress of Life.* Philadelphia: J. B. Lippincott, 1956.

Shealy, Norman. *Ninety Days to Self Health: Biogenics.* New York: Dial, 1977.

Simmel, Georg. *The Sociology of Georg Simmel*. New York: Glencoe Press, 1950.

————. "The Number of Members as Determining the Sociological Form of the Group." *American Journal of Sociology* VIII: 1 (July 1902) 45–46.

Simonton, Carl and Stephanie Simonton. *Getting Well Again.* New York: Bantam, 1980.

Watts, A. W. *Nature, Man and Woman.* New York: Pantheon Books, 1958.

————. *Psychotherapy East and West.* New York: Pantheon Books, 1961.

Watzlawick, P. *An Anthology of Human Communication.* Palo Alto: Science and Behavior Books, 1963.

————; J. Beavin; D. Jackson. *Pragmatics of Human Communication.* New York: W. W. Norton, 1967.

Wegscheider, Don. *If Only My Family Understood Me . . .* Minneapolis: CompCare Publications, 1979.

Wegscheider, Sharon. *Another Chance: Hope and Health for Alcoholic Families.* Palo Alto: Science and Behavior Books, 1981.

Whitaker, Carl and Augustus Y. Napier. *The Family Crucible: An Intensive Experience in Family Therapy.* New York: Harper & Row, 1978.

Index